T1-BJJ-003

NATIONS *of the* WORLD

SAMUEL BRIMSON

WORLD ALMANAC® LIBRARY

Please visit our web site at: www.worldalmanaclibrary.com
For a free color catalog describing World Almanac® Library's list
of high-quality books and multimedia programs, call 1-800-848-2928 (USA)
or 1-800-387-3178 (Canada). World Almanac® Library's fax: (414) 332-3567.

Library of Congress Cataloging-in-Publication Data available upon request from
publisher. Fax (414) 336-0157 for the attention of the Publishing Records Department.

ISBN 0-8368-5485-3

This North American edition first published in 2004 by
World Almanac® Library
330 West Olive Street, Suite 100
Milwaukee, WI 53212 USA

Created by Trocadero Publishing, an Electra Media Group Enterprise,
Suite 204, 74 Pitt Street, Sydney NSW 2000, Australia.

Original copyright © 2003 S. and L. Brodie.
This U.S. edition copyright © 2004 by World Almanac® Library.

World Almanac® Library editor: Gus Gedatus
Cover design: Scott M. Krall

Printed in Canada

1 2 3 4 5 6 7 8 9 07 06 05 04 03

Contents

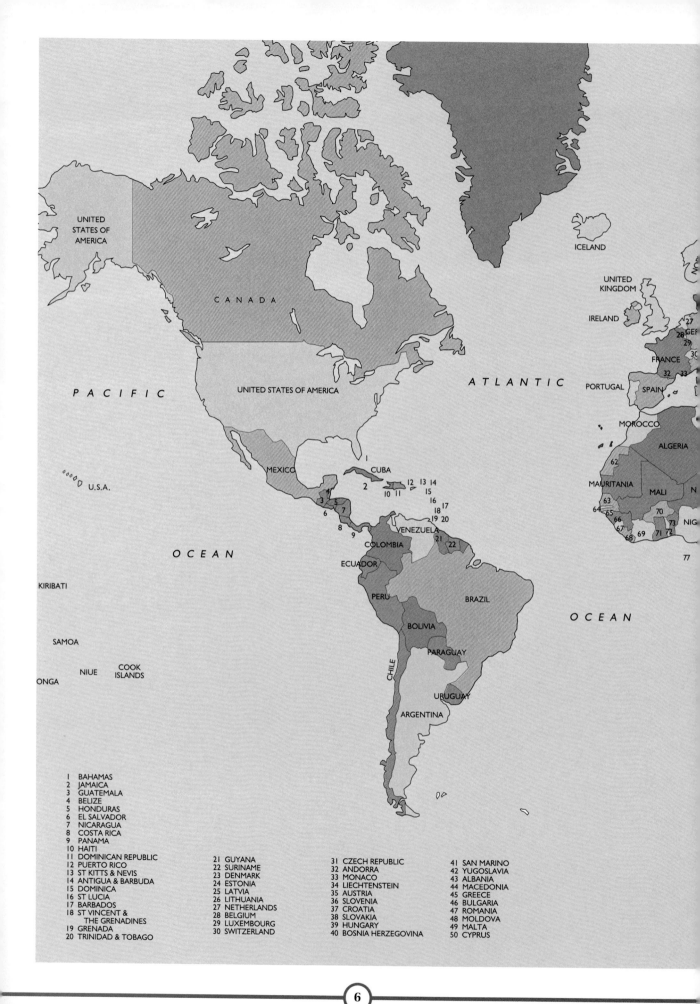

PACIFIC OCEAN

ATLANTIC OCEAN

UNITED STATES OF AMERICA

CANADA

ICELAND

UNITED KINGDOM

IRELAND

FRANCE

PORTUGAL
SPAIN

MOROCCO

ALGERIA

MAURITANIA

MALI

KIRIBATI

SAMOA

ONGA
NIUE
COOK ISLANDS

U.S.A.

MEXICO

CUBA

VENEZUELA

COLOMBIA

ECUADOR

PERU

BOLIVIA

PARAGUAY

CHILE

BRAZIL

URUGUAY

ARGENTINA

OCEAN

1 BAHAMAS
2 JAMAICA
3 GUATEMALA
4 BELIZE
5 HONDURAS
6 EL SALVADOR
7 NICARAGUA
8 COSTA RICA
9 PANAMA
10 HAITI
11 DOMINICAN REPUBLIC
12 PUERTO RICO
13 ST KITTS & NEVIS
14 ANTIGUA & BARBUDA
15 DOMINICA
16 ST LUCIA
17 BARBADOS
18 ST VINCENT &
      THE GRENADINES
19 GRENADA
20 TRINIDAD & TOBAGO

21 GUYANA
22 SURINAME
23 DENMARK
24 ESTONIA
25 LATVIA
26 LITHUANIA
27 NETHERLANDS
28 BELGIUM
29 LUXEMBOURG
30 SWITZERLAND

31 CZECH REPUBLIC
32 ANDORRA
33 MONACO
34 LIECHTENSTEIN
35 AUSTRIA
36 SLOVENIA
37 CROATIA
38 SLOVAKIA
39 HUNGARY
40 BOSNIA HERZEGOVINA

41 SAN MARINO
42 YUGOSLAVIA
43 ALBANIA
44 MACEDONIA
45 GREECE
46 BULGARIA
47 ROMANIA
48 MOLDOVA
49 MALTA
50 CYPRUS

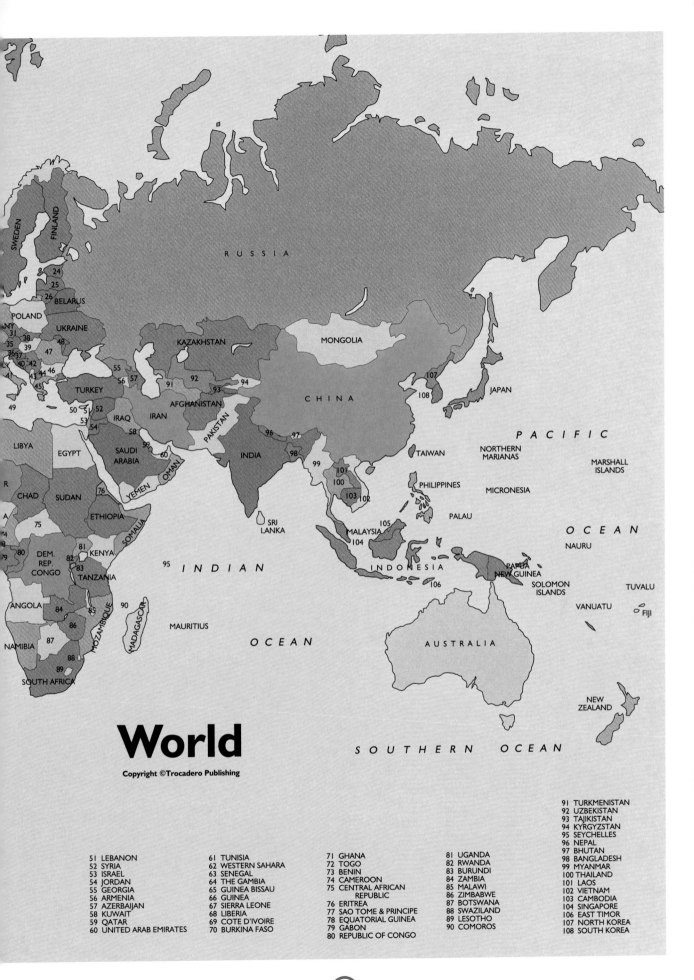

World

Copyright ©Trocadero Publishing

SWEDEN
FINLAND
24
25
26 BELARUS
POLAND
NY 31
35 39 48
36 37 47
40 42 44 46
41 45
TURKEY
49
50 51 52
53
54
LIBYA 58 59
EGYPT 60
SAUDI ARABIA
YEMEN OMAN
CHAD 76
SUDAN
ETHIOPIA
75
SOMALIA
80 81 82 KENYA
79 83
DEM. REP. CONGO
TANZANIA
95
ANGOLA 84 85 90
86
NAMIBIA 87
88
89
SOUTH AFRICA
MADAGASCAR
MOZAMBIQUE
MAURITIUS

UKRAINE
KAZAKHSTAN
55
56 57
91
92
93 94
AFGHANISTAN
IRAQ IRAN
PAKISTAN
INDIA
96 97
98
99 101
100
103 102
SRI LANKA
MALAYSIA 105
104
INDONESIA
106

RUSSIA
MONGOLIA
CHINA
107
108
JAPAN
TAIWAN

NORTHERN MARIANAS
PHILIPPINES
PALAU
MICRONESIA

PACIFIC
MARSHALL ISLANDS

OCEAN
NAURU

PAPUA NEW GUINEA
SOLOMON ISLANDS
TUVALU
VANUATU FIJI

INDIAN
OCEAN

AUSTRALIA

SOUTHERN OCEAN

NEW ZEALAND

51 LEBANON	61 TUNISIA	71 GHANA	81 UGANDA	91 TURKMENISTAN
52 SYRIA	62 WESTERN SAHARA	72 TOGO	82 RWANDA	92 UZBEKISTAN
53 ISRAEL	63 SENEGAL	73 BENIN	83 BURUNDI	93 TAJIKISTAN
54 JORDAN	64 THE GAMBIA	74 CAMEROON	84 ZAMBIA	94 KYRGYZSTAN
55 GEORGIA	65 GUINEA BISSAU	75 CENTRAL AFRICAN	85 MALAWI	95 SEYCHELLES
56 ARMENIA	66 GUINEA	REPUBLIC	86 ZIMBABWE	96 NEPAL
57 AZERBAIJAN	67 SIERRA LEONE	76 ERITREA	87 BOTSWANA	97 BHUTAN
58 KUWAIT	68 LIBERIA	77 SAO TOME & PRINCIPE	88 SWAZILAND	98 BANGLADESH
59 QATAR	69 COTE D'IVOIRE	78 EQUATORIAL GUINEA	89 LESOTHO	99 MYANMAR
60 UNITED ARAB EMIRATES	70 BURKINA FASO	79 GABON	90 COMOROS	100 THAILAND
		80 REPUBLIC OF CONGO		101 LAOS
				102 VIETNAM
				103 CAMBODIA
				104 SINGAPORE
				106 EAST TIMOR
				107 NORTH KOREA
				108 SOUTH KOREA

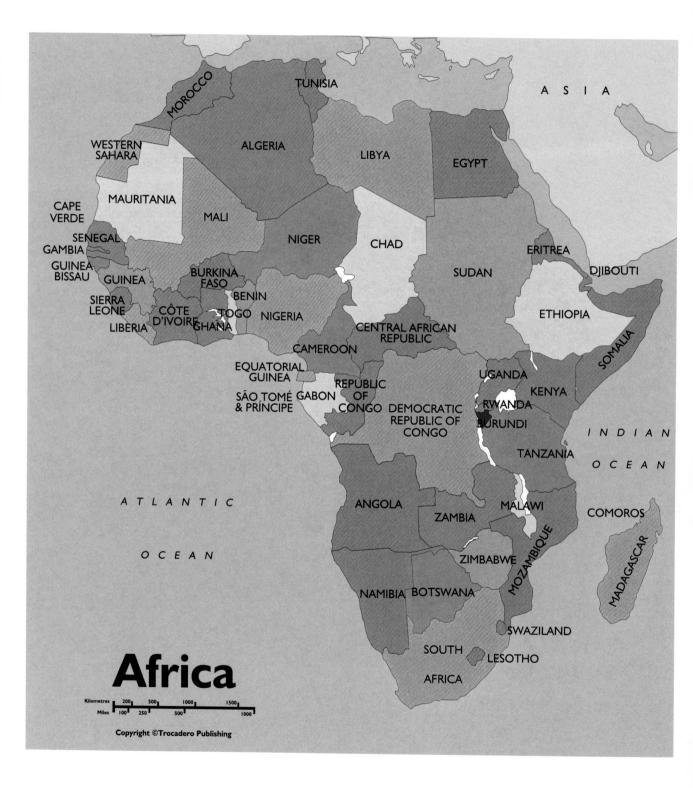

Africa

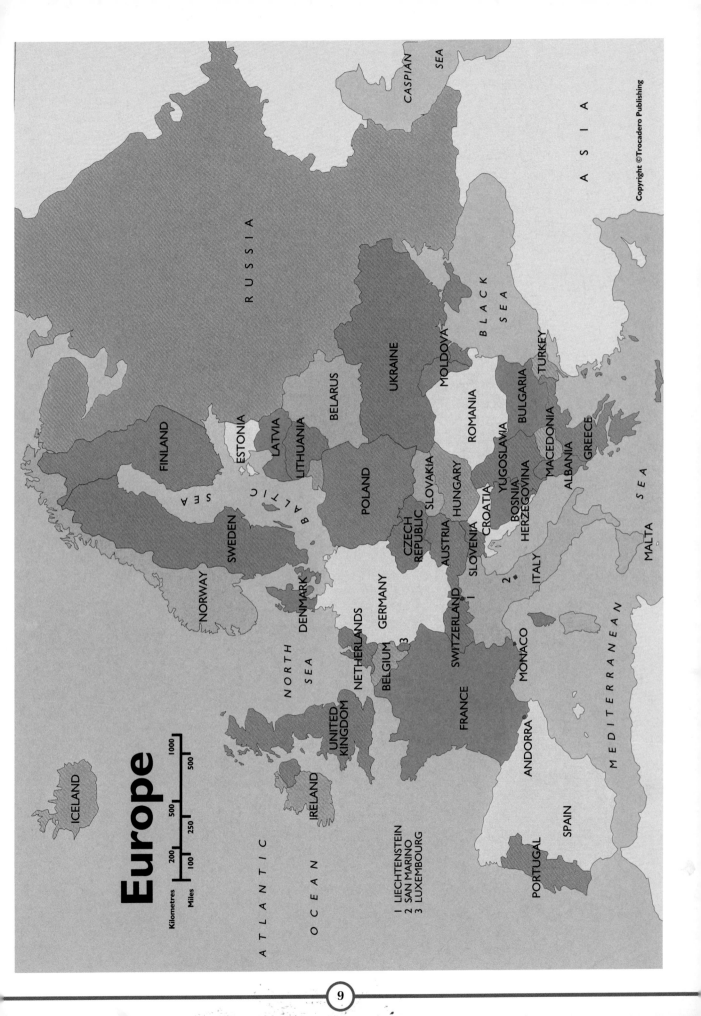

Europe

Kilometres
Miles

200
100
500
250
500
1000

1 LIECHTENSTEIN
2 SAN MARINO
3 LUXEMBOURG

ICELAND

IRELAND

UNITED KINGDOM

NORWAY

SWEDEN

FINLAND

ESTONIA

LATVIA

LITHUANIA

BELARUS

RUSSIA

UKRAINE

MOLDOVA

POLAND

DENMARK

NETHERLANDS

BELGIUM

GERMANY

CZECH REPUBLIC

SLOVAKIA

HUNGARY

AUSTRIA

SWITZERLAND

FRANCE

MONACO

ANDORRA

SPAIN

PORTUGAL

SLOVENIA

CROATIA

BOSNIA HERZEGOVINA

ITALY

YUGOSLAVIA

ROMANIA

BULGARIA

MACEDONIA

ALBANIA

GREECE

TURKEY

MALTA

ATLANTIC

OCEAN

NORTH SEA

BALTIC SEA

BLACK SEA

CASPIAN SEA

MEDITERRANEAN SEA

ASIA

1

2

3

North America
Central America

United States of America (upper left)

UNITED
STATES OF
AMERICA

*LABRADOR
SEA*

ATLANTIC

*HUDSON
BAY*

C A N A D A

PACIFIC

OCEAN

UNITED STATES OF AMERICA

1 SAINT KITTS AND NEVIS
2 ANTIGUA AND BARBUDA
3 DOMINICA
4 SAINT LUCIA
5 SAINT VINCENT AND GRENADINES
6 BARBADOS
7 GRENADA
8 TRINIDAD AND TOBAGO
9 TURKS AND CAICOS

OCEAN

*GULF
OF
MEXICO*

BAHAMAS

DOMINICAN
REPUBLIC

MEXICO

CUBA

HAITI

PUERTO
RICO

1 2
3
5 4 6
7
8

JAMAICA

CARIBBEAN   SEA

BELIZE
GUATEMALA HONDURAS
EL SALVADOR NICARAGUA
COSTA RICA PANAMA

| Kilometres | 500 | 1000 | 1500 |
| Miles | 500 | 1000 |

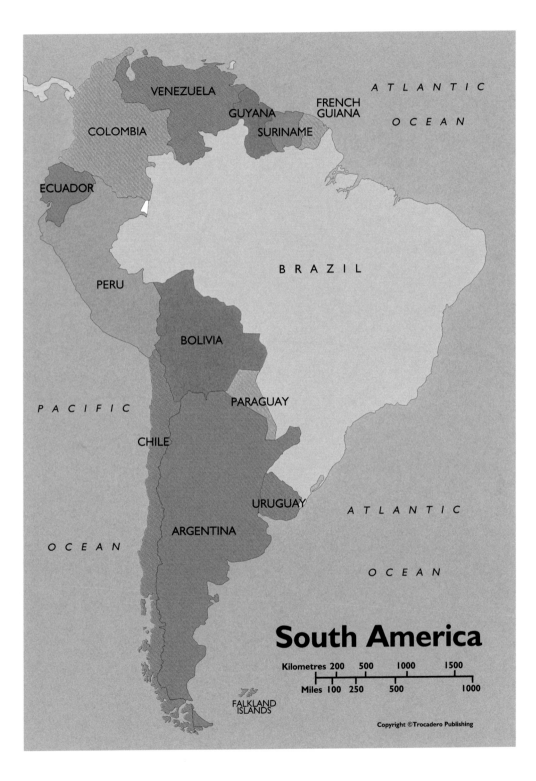

VENEZUELA

COLOMBIA

GUYANA

FRENCH
GUIANA

SURINAME

ATLANTIC

OCEAN

ECUADOR

PERU

BRAZIL

BOLIVIA

PARAGUAY

PACIFIC

CHILE

URUGUAY

ATLANTIC

ARGENTINA

OCEAN

OCEAN

FALKLAND
ISLANDS

South America

Kilometres 200 500 1000 1500

Miles 100 250 500 1000

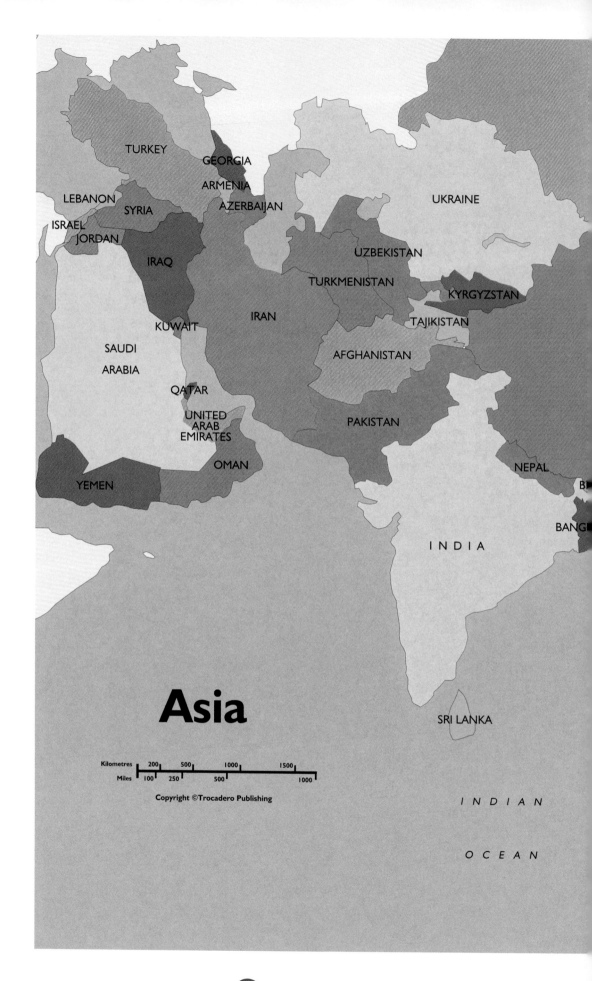

TURKEY

GEORGIA

ARMENIA

AZERBAIJAN

UKRAINE

LEBANON

SYRIA

ISRAEL
JORDAN

IRAQ

UZBEKISTAN

TURKMENISTAN

KYRGYZSTAN

KUWAIT

IRAN

TAJIKISTAN

SAUDI

ARABIA

AFGHANISTAN

QATAR

UNITED
ARAB
EMIRATES

PAKISTAN

OMAN

NEPAL

B

YEMEN

BANG

INDIA

Asia

SRI LANKA

Kilometres | 200 | 500 | 1000 | 1500

Miles | 100 | 250 | 500 | 1000

Copyright ©Trocadero Publishing

I N D I A N

O C E A N

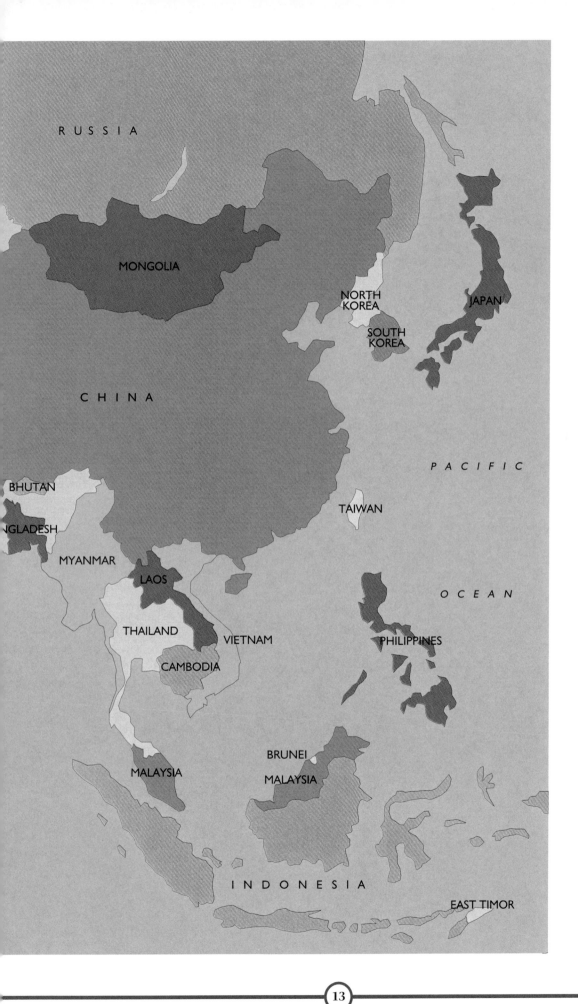

NORTHERN
MARIANAS

GUAM

MARSHALL

ISLANDS

PALAU

MICRONESIA

NAU

PAPUA

NEW GUINEA

SOLOMON
ISLANDS

VANUATU

NEW
CALEDONIA

AUSTRALIA

NEW Z

PACIFIC

LL
S

NAURU

KIRIBATI

TUVALU

SAMOA   AMERICAN
              SAMOA

U

FIJI   COOK   FRENCH

TONGA   NIUE   ISLANDS   POLYNESIA

W
ONIA

OCEAN

Pacific

EW ZEALAND

International organizations

AL	Arab League or League of Arab States
APEC	Asia-Pacific Economic Cooperation Forum
ASEAN	Association of South-East Asian Nations
Caricom	Caribbean Community and Common Market
CE	Council of Europe
CIS	Commonwealth of Independent States
CN	Commonwealth of Nations
EU	European Union
G-10	Group of 10 economic leaders
IMF	International Monetary Fund
NAFTA	North American Free Trade Agreement
NATO	North Atlantic Treaty Organization
OAS	Organization of American States
OAU	Organization of African Unity
OECD	Organization for Economic Cooperation and Development
OPEC	Organization of Petroleum Exporting Countries
SPF	South Pacific Forum
UN	United Nations
UNESCO	United Nations Economic, Scientific and Cultural Organization
UNHCR	United Nations High Commission for Refugees
WHO	World Health Organization
WTO	World Trade Organization

Arab League
Algeria
Bahrain
Comoros
Djibouti
Egypt
Iraq
Jordan
Kuwait
Lebanon
Libya
Mauritania
Morocco
Oman
Palestine
Qatar
Saudi Arabia
Somalia
Sudan
Syria
Tunisia
United Arab Emirates
Yemen

Asia-Pacific Economic Cooperation (APEC)
Australia
Brunei
Canada
Chile
China
Indonesia
Japan
South Korea
Malaysia
Mexico
New Zealand
Papua New Guinea
Peru
Philippines
Russia
Singapore
Taiwan
Thailand
United States of America
Vietnam

Association of South-East Asian Nations (ASEAN)
Brunei
Cambodia
Indonesia
Laos
Malaysia
Myanmar
Philippines
Singapore
Thailand
Vietnam

Caribbean Community and Common Market (Caricom)
Antigua and Barbuda
Bahamas
Barbados
Belize
Dominica
Grenada
Guyana
Haiti
Jamaica
Montserrat
Saint Kitts and Nevis
Saint Lucia
Saint Vincent and the Grenadines
Suriname
Trinidad and Tobago

Council of Europe (CE)
Albania
Andorra
Armenia
Austria
Azerbaijan
Belgium
Bosnia and Herzegovina
Bulgaria
Croatia
Cyprus
Czech Republic
Denmark
Estonia
Finland
France
Georgia
Germany
Greece
Hungary
Iceland
Ireland
Italy
Latvia
Liechtenstein
Lithuania
Luxembourg
Macedonia
Malta
Moldova
Netherlands
Norway
Poland
Portugal

Romania
Russia
San Marino
Slovakia
Slovenia
Spain
Sweden
Switzerland
Turkey
Ukraine
United Kingdom

Commonwealth of Independent States (CIS)

Azerbaijan
Armenia
Belarus
Kazakstan
Kyrgyzstan
Moldova
Russia
Tajikistan
Uzbekistan
Ukraine

Commonwealth of Nations (CN)

Antigua and Barbuda
Australia
Bahamas
Bangladesh
Barbados
Belize
Botswana
Brunei
Cameroon
Canada
Cyprus
Dominica
Fiji
The Gambia
Ghana
Grenada
Guyana
India
Jamaica
Kenya
Kiribati
Lesotho
Malawi
Malaysia
Maldives
Malta
Mauritius
Mozambique
Namibia
Nauru

New Zealand
Nigeria
Pakistan
Papua New Guinea
Samoa
Seychelles
Sierra Leone
Singapore
Solomon Islands
South Africa
Sri Lanka
Saint Kitts and Nevis
Saint Lucia
Saint Vincent and the Grenadines
Swaziland
Tanzania
Tonga
Trinidad and Tobago
Tuvalu
Uganda
United Kingdom
Vanuatu
Zambia
Zimbabwe

European Union (EU)

Austria
Belgium
Denmark
Finland
France
Germany
Greece
Ireland
Italy
Luxembourg
Netherlands
Portugal
Spain
Sweden
United Kingdom

North Atlantic Treaty Organization (NATO)

Belgium
Canada
Czech Republic
Denmark
France
Germany
Greece
Hungary
Iceland
Italy
Luxembourg
Netherlands
Norway

Poland
Portugal
Spain
Turkey
United Kingdom
United States of America

Organization of American States (OAS)

Antigua and Barbuda
Argentina
Bahamas
Barbados
Belize
Bolivia
Brazil
Canada
Chile
Colombia
Costa Rica
Cuba
Dominica
Dominican Republic
Ecuador
El Salvador
Grenada
Guatemala
Guyana
Haiti
Honduras
Jamaica
Mexico
Nicaragua
Panama
Paraguay
Peru
Saint Lucia
Saint Vincent and the Grenadines
Saint Kitts and Nevis
Suriname
Trinidad and Tobago
United States of America
Uruguay
Venezuela

Organization of African Unity (OAU)

Algeria
Angola
Benin
Botswana
Burkina Faso
Burundi
Cameroon
Cape Verde
Central African Republic

Chad
Comoros
Cote D'ivoire
Democratic Republic Of Congo
Djibouti
Egypt
Equatorial Guinea
Eritrea
Ethiopia
Gabon
Gambia
Ghana
Guinea
Guinea-Bissau
Kenya
Lesotho
Liberia
Libya
Madagascar
Malawi
Mali
Mauritania
Mauritius
Mozambique
Namibia
Niger
Nigeria
Rwanda
Sao Tome And Principe
Seychelles
Senegal
Sierra Leone
Somalia
South Africa
Sudan
Swaziland
Tanzania
TogoTunisia
Uganda
Zambia
Zimbabwe

Organization for Economic Cooperation and Development (OECD)

Australia
Austria
Belgium
Canada
Czech Republic
Denmark
Finland
France
Germany

Greece
Hungary
Iceland
Ireland
Italy
Japan
Korea
Luxembourg
Mexico
Netherlands
New Zealand
Norway
Poland
Portugal
Slovakia
Spain
Sweden
Switzerland
Turkey
United Kingdom
United States of America

Organization of Petroleum Exporting Countries (OPEC)

Algeria
Indonesia
Iran
Iraq
Kuwait
Libya
Nigeria
Qatar
Saudia Arabia
United Arab Emirates
Venezuela

South Pacific Forum

Australia
Cook Islands
Fiji
Kiribati
Marshall Islands
Micronesia
Nauru
New Zealand
Niue
Palau
Papua New Guinea
Samoa
Solomon Islands
Tonga
Tuvalu
Vanuatu

United Nations (UN)
Members and year of joining

Afghanistan 1946
Albania 1955
Algeria 1962
Andorra 1993
Angola 1976
Antigua and Barbuda 1981
Argentina 1945
Armenia 1992
Australia 1945
Austria 1955
Azerbaijan 1992
Bahamas 1973
Bahrain 1971
Bangladesh 1974
Barbados 1966
Belarus 1945
Belgium 1945
Belize 1981
Benin 1960
Bhutan 1971
Bolivia 1945
Bosnia and Herzegovina 1992
Botswana 1966
Brazil 1945
Brunei 1984
Bulgaria 1955
Burkina Faso 1960
Burundi 1962
Cambodia 1955
Cameroon 1960
Canada 1945
Cape Verde 1975
Central African Republic 1960
Chad 1960
Chile 1945
China 1945
Colombia 1945
Comoros 1975
Congo, Democratic Republic of the 1960
Congo, Republic of 1960
Costa Rica 1945
Côte d'Ivoire 1960
Croatia 1992
Cuba 1945
Cyprus 1960
Czech Republic 1993
Denmark 24 October 1945
Djibouti 20 September 1977
Dominica 1978
Dominican Republic 1945
Ecuador 1945
Egypt 1945

East Timor   2002
El Salvador   1945
Equatorial Guinea   1968
Eritrea   1993
Estonia   1991
Ethiopia   1945
Fiji   1970
Finland   1955
France   1945
Gabon   1960
Gambia   1965
Georgia   1992
Germany   1973
Ghana   1957
Greece   1945
Grenada   1974
Guatemala   1945
Guinea   1958
Guinea-Bissau   1974
Guyana   1966
Haiti   1945
Honduras   1945
Hungary   1955
Iceland   1946
India   1945
Indonesia   1950
Iran   1945
Iraq   1945
Ireland   1955
Israel   1949
Italy   1955
Jamaica   1962
Japan   1956
Jordan   1955
Kazakhstan   1992
Kenya   1963
Kiribati   1999
Korea, Democratic People's
    Republic of   1991
Korea, Republic of   1991
Kuwait   1963
Kyrgyzstan   1992
Laos   1955
Latvia   1991
Lebanon   1945
Lesotho   1966
Liberia   1945
Libya   1955
Liechtenstein   1990
Lithuania   1991
Luxembourg   24 October 1945
Macedonia   1993
Madagascar   1960
Malawi   1964
Malaysia   1957

Maldives   1965
Mali   1960
Malta   1964
Marshall Islands   1991
Mauritania   1961
Mauritius   1968
Mexico   1945
Micronesia   1991
Moldova   1992
Monaco   1993
Mongolia   1961
Morocco   1956
Mozambique   1975
Myanmar   1948
Namibia   1990
Nauru   1999
Nepal   1955
Netherlands   1945
New Zealand   1945
Nicaragua   1945
Niger   1960
Nigeria   1960
Norway   1945
Oman   1971
Pakistan   1947
Palau   1994
Panama   1945
Papua New Guinea   1975
Paraguay   1945
Peru   1945
Philippines   1945
Poland   1945
Portugal   1955
Qatar   1971
Romania   1955
Russia   1945
Rwanda   1962
Saint Kitts and Nevis   1983
Saint Lucia   1979
Saint Vincent and the Grenadines
    1980
Samoa   1976
San Marino   1992
Sao Tome and Principe   1975
Saudi Arabia   1945
Senegal   1960
Seychelles   1976
Sierra Leone   27 September 1961
Singapore   21 September 1965
Slovakia   19 January 1993
Slovenia   22 May 1992
Solomon Islands   1978
Somalia   1960
South Africa   1945
Spain   1955

Sri Lanka   1955
Sudan   1956
Suriname   1975
Swaziland   1968
Sweden   1946
Switzerland   2002
Syrian Arab Republic   1945
Tajikistan   1992
Tanzania   1961
Thailand   1946
Togo   1960
Tonga   1999
Trinidad and Tobago   1962
Tunisia   1956
Turkey   1945
Turkmenistan   1992
Tuvalu   2000
Uganda   1962
Ukraine   1945
United Arab Emirates   1971
United Kingdom of Great Britain
    and Northern Ireland   1945
United States of America   1945
Uruguay   1945
Uzbekistan   1992
Vanuatu   1981
Venezuela   1945
Vietnam   1977
Yemen   1947
Yugoslavia   2000
Zambia   1964
Zimbabwe   1980

Afghanistan

ISLAMIC REPUBLIC OF AFGHANISTAN

GOVERNMENT
Capital Kabul
Type of government
Afghan Interim Authority (AIA) transitional
Independence from British influence
August 19, 1919
Voting to be determined
Head of state Chairman of AIA
Head of government
Chairman of AIA
Constitution Being drafted
Legislature Suspended
Judiciary
Supreme Court to be created
Member of IMF, OECD, UN, UNESCO, WHO

LAND AND PEOPLE
Land area 250,000 sq mi (647,500 sq km)
Highest point
Nowshak 24,557 ft (7485 m)
Population 27,755,000
Major cities and populations
Kabul 2 million
Kandahar 0.3 million
Massar-e Sharif 0.3 million
Ethnic groups
Pashtun, Tajik, Uzbek, Hazara
Religions
Islam 98%, Judaism 1%, Hinduism 1%
Languages Pashto, Dari

ECONOMIC
Currency Afghani
Industries
textiles, footwear, carpets, coal, copper, natural gas
Agriculture
wheat, fruits, nuts, wool, mutton, other sheep products
Natural resources
natural gas, petroleum, coal, copper, chromite, sulphur, lead, zinc, iron ore

Afghanistan, a landlocked country in western central Asia, is situated high above sea level. About four-fifths of its land is mountains, ranging from over 4000 feet (1216 m) to 25,000 feet (7622 m) high. The central highlands, which include the Hindu Kush range, make up more than half of the country. Most of the people of Afghanistan live in the deep, narrow valleys of the Hindu Kush Mountains. The climate throughout the country is harsh, varying from bitterly cold winters to hot, dry summers.

More than half the people of Afghanistan are Pashtuns, who dominate the east and south. The Pashtun's speak a language called Pashto, one of Afghanistan's official languages. Tajiks live in the northwest, particularly around Herat. These people speak Dari, the country's other official language. Smaller but significant ethnic groups include the Uzbeks and the Hazaras.

Religion has played a major role in Afghanistan's history. Most of the people are Sunni Muslims, while just over ten percent are Shi'ites. There are very small numbers of Hindus and Sikhs, as well as a tiny Jewish minority.

Because of the devastation of consistent wars, Afghanistan does not have many good schools. Less than fifty percent of the country's males and about fifteen percent of its females are able to read. During the Taliban control of the 1990s, all females were banned from schools.

The economy of Afghanistan has been devastated by two decades of war. Mining, agriculture, and manufacturing have been greatly impaired since the 1980s. This occurred largely because of damage to paved roads essential for transporting products.

Most of Afghanistan's people earn their living from agriculture. Wheat, cotton, beet sugar, nuts, and fruits are the main crops. Fat-tailed sheep supply food as well as wool and skins for clothing. Farming is difficult, due to a shortage of modern equipment as well as serious periods of drought in recent years. At the present time, very few farm products are exported.

During the 1980s and '90s, Afghanistan became a major producer of opium, which is used to make heroin, an illegal drug. Many farmers grew opium poppies instead of food crops to make large, fast profits. Efforts are being made to control opium production in the country, while improving production of food crops.

Most of Afghanistan's manufacturing takes place in homes and small shops. Artisans cre-

ate textiles, footwear, and beautiful carpets. Afghan rugs are among some of the country's more impressive exports.

Afghanistan exports a significant amount of natural gas. Coal mining also provides some income. However, large deposits of iron ore, precious metals, and various gemstones have not been exploited for many years.

Historians believe that civilizations were established in southern Afghanistan during prehistoric times. The region was conquered by King Darius I of Persia around 500 B.C., but fell to Alexander the Great in 329 B.C. In the second century B.C., Buddhists established the Kushan dynasty, which lasted until the third century A.D. when the Sassanids took power.

Islam was introduced in the seventh century A.D. Over the next 400 years several Muslim dynasties prospered, then collapsed. Turkish Sultan Mahmud of Ghazni conquered Afghanistan in the eleventh century, followed by Mongol Genghis Khan, then the Timur, or Tamerlane, dynasty.

Beginning in 1747, Persian ruler Ahmad Shah united much of present-day Afghanistan. This period was considered the beginning of an Afghan state.

Ahmad Shah's Durrani dynasty collapsed in 1818.

Both Britain and Russia wanted to control the northern access routes from Afghanistan to India. In 1838, Britain invaded Afghanistan, beginning the first Afghan War, which lasted for four years. During the following decades, Britain had a varying control over the country. A second Afghan War took place in 1878, but this conflict lasted

less than a year. In 1919, to escape British influence altogether, Emir Amanullah began the third Afghan War. It ended with Afghanistan gaining full independence.

Amanullah reduced the power of religious leaders and introduced a more liberal regime for women. This led to his removal and replacement by Nadir Shah in 1929. Nadir Shah continued the process

Children in a United Nations refugee camp.

Afghanistan

of modernization until he was assassinated in 1933.

From the 1940s to the 1970s neutral Afghanistan maintained relations with the United States and the Soviet Union. An economic crisis saw King Muhammad Zahir Shah deposed by the military in July of 1973. A republic was proclaimed, with Muhammad Daoud Khan as president. In 1978, during yet another takeover, Daoud was killed.

A Revolutionary Council, led by Noor Mohammed Taraki, took control. This group suspended the constitution in lieu of a new type of government similar to communism. Devout Muslims felt that such a system conflicted with Islam. Opposition to reform led to invasion by Soviet troops. Soviet Babrak Karmal became president.

Anti-Soviet Afghans formed the Mujahadin, or "holy warriors." With considerable United States support, they fought a ten-year guerilla war against the Soviets beginning in 1979. The conflict took thousands of lives and badly harmed the nation's economy before the Soviet Union withdrew its troops in 1989.

By 1992 the guerrillas had established a new government. However, disagreements led to weak, divisive leadership. In 1994, a powerful group of Islamic Pashtuns called the Taliban seized power. These people insisted that Afghans follow the strictest precepts of Islam.

FLAT EARTH PICTURE GALLERY

Continuing conflict involved all parts of Afghan society, including this teenage boy with his automatic rifle.

Those who did not obey the Taliban's rules were massacred.

In August 1998 the United States launched a missile attack on a suspected terrorist training camp outside Kabul. According to sources, this camp had been developed by Osama bin Laden, the man believed responsible for bombing U. S. embassies in Kenya and Tanzania. When the Taliban refusal to hand over Osama bin Laden, the United Nations imposed economic sanctions. By 2001 more than three million Afghans had fled to Pakistan and Iran. More than one million others had died in the fighting.

Afghanistan came into international focus on September 11, 2001, following attacks on New York and Washington D.C. Believing the attacks were led by Osama bin Laden, international forces, dominated by the United States, attacked Taliban strongholds in the country. By 2002 the Taliban had been deposed and replaced by a more liberal regime. Efforts to establish a unified nation continue. As of spring, 2003, attempts to capture Osama bin Laden have been unsuccessful.

Albania

REPUBLIC OF ALBANIA

GOVERNMENT
Capital Tirana
Type of government
Republic
**Independence from
Ottoman Empire**
November 12, 1912
Voting
universal adult suffrage, compulsory
Head of state President
Head of government Prime
Minister
Constitution 1991
Legislature
Elected unicameral people's
assembly
(Kuvendi Popullor)
Judiciary Supreme Court
Member of CE, IMF, UN,
UNESCO, WHO, WTO

LAND AND PEOPLE
Land area 11,200 sq mi
(28,748 sq km)
Highest point Mt. Korabit
9,026 ft (2751 m)
Coastline 225 mi (362 km)
Population 3,544,841
Major cities and populations
Tirana 250,000
Durrës 86,000
Elbasan 84,000
Ethnic groups
Albanian 95%, Greek 3%
Religions Islam 70%,
Christianity 30%
Language Albanian (official)

ECONOMIC
Currency Albanian lek
Industries
food processing, textiles, clothing,
timber, oil, cement, chemicals,
mining, hydroelectricitry
Agriculture
wheat, maize, potatoes, vegetables,
fruits, beet sugar, grapes, meat,
dairy
Natural resources
petroleum, natural gas, coal,
chromium, copper, timber, nickel

Albania is located on the eastern shores of the Adriatic Sea. Inland, the countryside becomes mountainous, with its highest point on the border with Macedonia. More than thirty percent of Albania is either heavily forested or swampy. The coastal climate is Mediterranean, with warm, dry summers and mild, wet winters. The inland experiences extreme cold during winter.

About ninety-five percent of the population is Albanian. Most of the rest are Greek. About seventy percent of Albanians are Muslim, while most of the remainder are Christian. Between 1967 and 1990, the Albanian government outlawed religious institutions. Since that time, however, religions have flourished. Albanian is the official language, with two main dialects, Gheg in the north and Tosk in the south. About 95 percent of Albanians can read.

Illyrian tribespeople were early inhabitants of the area, with a civilization at its height between 750 and 450 B.C. In 168 B.C. the land became the Roman province of Illyricum.

Roman control ended at the end of the fourth century A.D. Illyricum became part of the Byzantine Empire, though at various times it was also controlled by Serbia or Bulgaria. The Ottoman Empire took over in the fourteenth century, forcibly converting much of the population to Islam. It retained control until 1912.

Between 1912 and 1920, foreign powers occupied the country. An independent government, set up in 1921, attempted to make democracy work. Ahmet Zogu became its first president. However, in 1928, he declared himself King Zog I and ruled until the onset of World War II. During the war (1939-1944), Albania was occupied first by the Italians, then by the Germans.

A communist republic, led by Enver Hoxha, was formed in 1946, beginning forty years of harsh dictatorship. But in the late 1980s, as other parts of Europe abandoned communism, Albanians wanted change, too. Demonstrators clashed with police in 1990, as refugees began pouring out of the country.

The communists were defeated in the 1992 elections. Sali Berisha became the first democratically elected president. Unfortunately, in 1997 many Albanians suffered huge losses during a major financial crisis. This brought the country into chaos so severe than a U. N. peace-keeping force was called in. The Socialists won power in July 1997 and again in 2001, yet Democrats remain determined. Albania's economy is still in recovery and unemployment is high.

Algeria

THE PEOPLE'S DEMOCRATIC AND POPULAR REPUBLIC OF ALGERIA

Algeria is located on the Mediterranean coast of northwestern Africa. The fertile coastal plain, where about ninety percent of the country's people live, gives way to a more arid landscape near the Atlas Mountains. Farther south, covering about four-fifths of the country, is the Algerian Sahara Desert. Coastal winters are cool and wet. Summers are hot and dry. In the desert, temperature ranges are particularly extreme.

The population is largely of Arab–Berber descent. Islam is the state religion but there are small Christian and Jewish communities. Arabic is Algeria's official language, but about fifteen percent of the population speak Tamazight while others speak French.

Berbers inhabited the region for over 5,000 years. Roman colonizers named it Numidia in 106 B.C. In 429 A.D. the Vandals invaded, creating chaos until the Byzantine Empire exerted control in the sixth century A.D. Soon, Arab traders began arriving, bringing Islam. The Ottoman Empire annexed Algeria in the mid-sixteenth century.

France invaded in 1830, facing stiff resistance before taking complete control in 1848. After World War I, Algerian nationalist movements wanted either integration with France or independence. Failure to win equality with the French led

Algerians to feel that independence was essential.

The National Liberation Front (FLN) staged a relentless guerrilla war against French troops during the 1950s. When Charles DeGaulle became president in the late '50s, he permitted Algerians to vote on independence. On July 3, 1962, Algeria was declared an independent country.

President Ahmed Ben Bella nationalized industries and seized European-owned farms. He was deposed by Colonel Houari Boumedienne in 1965. For two decades, the FLN was Algeria's sole political party.

Unrest, driven by a poor economy, ended the one-party state in 1989. The Islamic Salvation Front (FIS) dominated provincial and municipal elections. President Chadli Bendjedid responded by arresting many of its members.

When the FIS won a sweeping victory in December 1991, the military declared a state of emergency. By 1995 assassinations and bombings were commonplace and 100,000 people had died. The situation eased when Abdelaziz Bouteflika became president in 1999. After the September 11, 2001, attacks on the United States, Algeria offered to turn over resident members of the al-Qaeda network who were believed to be supporters of terrorist mastermind Osama bin Laden.

GOVERNMENT
Website www.algeria.com
Capital Algiers
Type of government
Republic
Independence from France
July 3, 1962
Voting Universal adult suffrage
Head of state President
Head of government Prime Minister
Constitution 1976
revised 1988, 1989, 1996
Legislature
Bicameral parliament
National People's Assembly
(lower house), National Council (upper house)
Judiciary Supreme Court
Member of AL, IMF, OAU, OECD, OPEC, UN, UNESCO, UNHCR, WHO

LAND AND PEOPLE
Land area 919,595 sq mi
(2,381,740 sq km)
Highest point Mt. Tahat 2918 m
(3003 m)
Coastline 725 mi (1,167 km)
Population 32,277,942
Major cities and populations
Algiers 1.7 million
Oran 0.7 million
Constantine 0.5 million
Ethnic groups Arab Berber
Religions Islam 99%
Languages Arabic (official), Berber

ECONOMIC
Currency Algerian dinar
Industry
petroleum, natural gas, mining, electrical, petrochemical, food processing
Agriculture
wheat, barley, oats, grapes, olives, citrus, fruits; sheep, cattle
Natural resources
petroleum, natural gas, iron ore, phosphates, uranium, lead, zinc

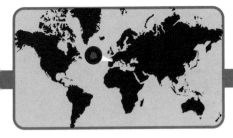

Andorra

PRINCIPALITY OF ANDORRA

GOVERNMENT
Website www.andorra.ad
Capital Andorra la Vella
Type of government
Parliamentary democracy
Voting Universal adult suffrage
Head of state
President of France and
Bishop of See de Urgel (jointly)
Head of government Prime
Minister
Constitution 1993
Legislature
Unicameral
General Council of the Valleys
Judiciary Tribunal of Judges
Member of CE, UN, UNESCO,
WHO

LAND AND PEOPLE
Land area 181 sq mi (464 sq km)
Highest point Coma Pedrosa
9,665 mi (2,946 m)
Population 68,403
Major cities and populations
Andorra la Vella 22,000
Ethnic groups Spanish 60%,
Catalan 30%, French 6%
Religions Christianity
Languages Catalan (official)

ECONOMIC
Currency Euro
Industry
tourism, cattle, timber, banking
Agriculture
tobacco, rye, wheat, barley, oats,
vegetables, sheep, cattle
Natural resources
mineral waters, timber, iron ore,
lead

Andorra is a tiny country of just 181 square miles (464 sq km). It is located in the eastern Pyrenees Mountains on the border between France and Spain. The landscape is mountainous, with several deep valleys. The climate is cold in winter, with heavy snowfalls. In contrast, summers can be warm and pleasant. The geography is ideal for hydroelectric production, creating energy which is sold to Spain.

Sixty percent of the Andorran people are Spanish, twenty-five percent are Catalan, and six percent French. Most Andorrans earn their living from tourism, while a much smaller number work as farmers. Andorra's very low tax structure is attracting investors from other countries, so more and more people are working in financial services.

Andorra was created as a self-governing region in the ninth century A.D. Charles II, the Holy Roman Emperor, placed it under the control of the Count of Foix in 843. This was challenged by the Spanish Catholic Church, which claimed Andorra as its own territory. It took three hundred years to reach a solution. The country was placed under the joint control of the Count of Foix and the Spanish Catholic Bishop of See de Urgel.

In the sixteenth century, the Count of Foix's share passed to the King of France. As a result of the French Revolution, French control was terminated in 1793. Napoleon restored the arrangement in 1806, following requests from the Andorrans.

Subsequently, the country was ruled mainly by a group of long-established Andorran families. In 1993 it became a parliamentary democracy with an elected prime minister as head of government. The role of head of state is shared by the president of France and the Bishop of See de Urgel.

Andorra's beautiful mountainous landscape.

FLAT EARTH PICTURE GALLERY

Angola

REPUBLIC OF ANGOLA

Angola is located in southern Africa, with the Atlantic Ocean to the west. Inland from the coastal plain is a high plateau which covers much of southern Africa. Most of Angola is grassland, but there are also large tracts of dense forest. The Cuanza and Cunene are two major rivers which drain to the Atlantic Ocean. October through March is the rainy season. The climate is tropical, with high temperatures throughout the year.

The population of Angola is made up of more than 90 ethnic groups. The people are primarily of Ovimbundu, Kimbindu, and Bakongo origin. A small number are of a mixed European and Native African descent. Traditional indigenous religions are still practiced, but Christianity is widespread. Portuguese is the official language. Most people Bantu dialects.

Khoisan-speaking hunters and gatherers, often known as Bushmen, were the first inhabitants of what is now Angola. They were displaced in the seventh century A.D. by Bantu-speaking peoples. Several other kingdoms developed, including that of the Chokwe people.

Portuguese invaders colonized Angola in 1575, mainly as a source of slaves for its Brazilian colony. Many people resisted the brutal Portuguese control. Portugal attempted to impose their rule through appointed governors. This led to nearly constant warfare with the native people. The invaders did not gain complete dominance until 1902.

Independence movements such as the National Front for the Liberation of Angola (FNLA), the Popular Liberation Movement of Angola (MPLA) and National Union for the Total Independence of Angola (UNITA) arose in the 1960s. The groups waged ongoing guerrilla war against the 50,000 Portuguese troops stationed in the country. Following the collapse of Portugal's own government, Angola gained its independence in 1975.

The MPLA took control, opposed by FNLA and UNITA. Aid for the MPLA flowed in from the Soviet Union and Cuba. FNLA withered, but UNITA gained support from the United States and South Africa. A peace accord was reached in 1991, but disputed election results in 1992 provoked new fighting. United Nations peacekeepers arrived in 1995.

The situation today remains unresolved. UNITA continues its guerrilla war funded by the lucrative diamond mines it controls. Decades of war have left most Angolans desperately poor. Revenue from exports of oil and diamonds is diverted to fund the armed forces, or lost in corrupt transactions.

GOVERNMENT
Website www.angola.org
Capital Luanda
Type of government
Presidential republic
Independence from Portugal
November 11, 1975
Voting Universal adult suffrage
Head of state President
Head of government President
Constitution 1975
revised 1978, 1980, 1991, 1992
Legislature
Unicameral National Assembly
Judiciary Supreme Court
Member of IMF, OAU, UN,
UNESCO, WHO, WTO

LAND AND PEOPLE
Land area 481,354 sq mi (1,246,700 sq km)
Highest point Morro de Moco
8,595 ft (2620 m)
Coastline 994 mi (600 km)
Population 10,593,171
Major cities and populations
Luanda 2,100,000
Huambo 225,000
Benguela 180,000
Lobito 170,000
Ethnic groups
Ovimbundu, Bakongo, Kimbundu
Religions
Christianity 65%,
indigenous faiths 35%
Languages Portuguese (official),
various Bantu dialects

ECONOMIC
Currency kwanza
Industry
petroleum, mining, cement, metal products, food processing, sugar, textiles
Agriculture
bananas, sugar cane, coffee, sisal, corn, cotton, tapioca, vegetables, livestock, timber, fish
Natural resources
diamonds, iron ore, phosphates, bauxite, uranium, gold, petroleum

Antigua and Barbuda

Three Caribbean islands, Antigua, Barbuda, and Redonda, make up the small nation of Antigua and Barbuda. All are in the eastern Caribbean Sea about 430 miles (692 km) north of Venezuela. Antigua is hilly and rugged, an ancient volcano worn down by wind and water. Barbuda is a flat coral island of beautiful sandy beaches. Redonda, a tiny, rocky islet, has little plant life and no people live there.

The climate is tropical but sea breezes usually make it pleasant. Annually, the islands receive an average of 45 inches (114 cm) of rain. However, in some years serious droughts have affected farming and island wildlife.

The people are primarily descended from Africans brought to the region as slaves to work on plantations. Christianity is the main religion. English is the official language.

Most people work in the tourism industry or in financial services. Antigua and Barbuda is a rapidly developing offshore banking center.

Antigua was visited and named by Christopher Columbus in 1493. The British colonized the island in 1632. Settlers colonized Barbuda in 1661.

Antigua soon developed a substantial sugar cane industry. The profitability of the plantations was built on the free labor of slaves. Captured Africans were imported to work the fields. Britain abolished slavery in the 1830s. The sugar industry then began a long decline. Sugar cane is still grown on the islands, but on a much smaller scale.

Internal self-government began with the formation of the Antigua Trades and Labor Union (ATL) in the 1940s. On November 1, 1981, the nation won independence from Britain and established itself as a parliamentary democracy.

The first prime minister, Vere Bird, had been president of the ATL for many years. Except for a short time in the 1970s, he was president of the country until 1989, when his son, Lester, was elected.

The country was named by the Organization for Economic Cooperation and Development (OECD) as one of thirty-five that are tax havens outside international guidelines. This has led to banking activities which have caused international concern, specifically in the United States and Britain. Questions have arisen about possible money laundering and involvement in drug trade.

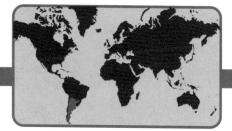

Argentina

The Plaza del Congreso in Buenos Aires, home of Argentina's parliament

BRAND X PICTURES

Argentina occupies much of the southern part of the South American continent. It stretches 2,300 miles (3700 km) from north to south. In the east it is bounded by the Atlantic Ocean. Its long western border with Chile follows the peaks of the Andes Mountains.

Geographically, Argentina is truly varied. Much of the Paraná Plateau in the northeast is densely forested. In the northwest, regions such as Gran Chaco and Mesopotamia have flat plains which often flood severely. South of this lie the flat grasslands of the immense Pampa, which stretches from the ocean in the east to the foothills of the Andes Mountains in the west. The Pampa is excellent land for farming, because it has the richest soil in the South America. Argentina's southernmost area is Patagonia, which is bleak and cold, although spectacular in places.

Argentina has a wide variety of climates, from the sub-tropical north to the bleak, freezing winters of Patagonia in the south. Temperatures in the Andes can fall to -4°F (-20 ° C) at night. Eastern cities such as Buenos Aires have cool winters and warm to hot summers. Rainfall is sparse in the west, but moderate to heavy in the eastern and northern regions.

Unlike most other South American countries,

28

Argentina's population is primarily descended from immigrants. Indigenous cultures were overrun and, in some places, wiped out by sustained immigration from Europe in the nineteenth and twentieth centuries. Most Argentinians are descended from Spanish or Italian families. Others have British, Swiss, German, French or Eastern European heritage. Most indigenous peoples live in the north and northwest.

Argentina is predominantly Roman Catholic, with some Protestants and those who practice the Eastern Orthodox faith. Argentina is also home to one of the largest Jewish populations in the world. As in most South American nations, the Catholic Church has a profound influence on many aspects of daily life.

At the beginning of the twentieth century, Argentina was one of the wealthiest countries in the world. It was believed to have the highest standard of living in South America. Subsequently, corrupt governments and economic mismanagement have considerably diminished its prosperity.

From the 1880s onward, a flood of migrants from Europe developed the vast Pampa region into one of the world's finest beef cattle production centers. Sheep, too, are raised for meat and wool. Argentina is also a major world producer of wheat.

Other crops include beet sugar, sorghum and soybeans. While not a major exporter of minerals, Argentina has oil and natural gas reserves sufficient for national requirements.

Throughout the twentieth century governments encouraged the development of heavy industries protected by import tariffs. This made the country self-sufficient for most of its consumer goods. Many industries were state-owned until the 1990s when the government began a program of privatization. Economic reforms introduced at the same period created a boom economy for a time.

The Argentine constitution was adopted in 1853 and modified in 1898 and 1994. The country has a federal system of government, consisting of a federal district centered on Buenos Aires, 22 provinces, and one territory. Its president is elected directly by the people for a four-year term and can only be reelected once. The National Congress is bicameral, with an upper house of 72 senators, and a lower house containing 257 deputies. Senators serve for six years, deputies for four years. Each province also has an elected governor and legislature.

As early as 10,000 B.C., small tribes of hunter-gatherers were established in the region that would become Argentina.

GOVERNMENT
Website www.info.gov.ar
Capital Buenos Aires
Type of government Republic
Independence from Spain
July 9, 1816
Voting
Universal adult suffrage, compulsory
Head of state President
Head of government President
Constitution 1853, revised 1994
Legislature
Bicameral National Congress
Chamber of Deputies (lower house)
Senate (upper house)
Judiciary Supreme Court
Member of IMF, OAS, UN,
UNESCO, UNHCR, WHO, WTO

LAND AND PEOPLE
Land area 1,072,163 sq mi
(2,776,800 sq km)
Highest point
Cerro Aconcagua 22,834 ft (6960 m)
Coastline 3100 mi (4989 km)
Population 37,812,817
Major cities and populations
Buenos Aires 13 million
Córdoba 1.5 million
Rosario 1.4 million
Mendoza 1 million
La Plata 0.8 million
Ethnic groups European 97%,
indigenous and mestizo 3%
Religions
Christianity 95%, Judaism 2%,
others 3%
Languages Spanish (official),
various indigenous languages

ECONOMIC
Currency Argentine peso
Industry
food processing, motor vehicles,
consumer goods, textiles, chemicals,
petrochemicals, steel
Agriculture
sunflower, fruits, soybeans, grapes,
corn, peanuts, tea, wheat, cattle
Natural resources
lead, zinc, tin, copper, iron ore,
manganese, petroleum, uranium

Argentina

FLAT EARTH PICTURE GALLERY

Colorful houses in the Camintinas la Boca district of Buenos Aires.

Formal tribal groupings, mostly farmers, emerged around 500 B.C. The lives of these people changed dramatically with the arrival of the Spanish in 1516.

Colonizers, led by Pedro de Mendoza, established a settlement at Buenos Aires and quickly began taking land from the indigenous people. Bloody clashes between the colonizers and the nomadic tribes of the west continued for many years. It was not until the nineteenth century that Spain finally overcame all opposition.

Initially Argentina was a part of Spain's Viceroyalty of Peru. In 1776 Argentina, Paraguay, Uruguay and Bolivia were incorporated into the new Viceroyalty of Río de la Plata. Buenos Aires was its administrative center.

When a British military force attacked Buenos Aires in 1806, the Spanish viceroy fled. However, Spanish loyalists led by Jacques de Liniers organized a resistance movement, which drove out the British that year and again in 1807.

In 1808, Napoleon Bonaparte of France deposed Spain's King Ferdinand VII. Argentine revolutionaries, who didn't want to be controlled by France, overthrew the viceroy on May 25, 1810. War erupted with royalists who sought a return to Spanish rule. Under the leadership of Manuel Belgrano, the revolutionaries won a major victory at Tucumán in 1812.

Former Spanish army officer, Jose de San Martin, returned to his Argentine birthplace to join the revolutinaries. He was determined to help rid South America of Spanish control. After several successful battles, his revolutionary army prevailed. On July 9, 1816, the Congress of Tucumán declared the United Provinces of Río de la Plata independent from Spain. Uruguay and Paraguay then opted to split from the new grouping. Jose de San Martin, who became known as "the liberator of Argentina," went on to lead successful independence movements in Chile and Peru.

Almost immediately, conflict erupted between the government in Buenos Aires and the people of the provinces. Provincial political leaders refused to surrender their considerable power and autonomy to the central government.

From 1835, until he was deposed in 1852, dictator Juan Manuel de Rosas brought some stability to the country. In 1853, a new constitution based on federal principles provoked a civil war between Buenos Aires and the provinces. Buenos Aires won the Battle of Pavón in 1861 and military leader Bartolomé Mitre became the first truly national president the following year.

During the rest of the nineteenth century a series of Argentinian presidents pacified and united their country. A program was launched to attract foreign investors and immigrants from Europe in the 1880s. People were arriving at the rate of 200,000 per year, the largest number coming from Italy, within a short time.

British investors poured vast sums into Argentina. The railway system was expanded from 1,864 miles (3000 km) to more than 19,500 miles (32,000 km). This opened the vast Pampa up to beef cattle production and the cultivation of grains and cereals. The area of farmed land increased from 2.5 million acres (1 million ha) in 1860 to 59.3 million acres (24 million ha) in 1910. Refrigerated shipping enabled the export of meat to European markets.

Because only landowners could vote, political power remained firmly in the hands of business and farming interests in the Conservative Party. However, in 1890 the Radical Civic Union (UCR) was formed to represent the middle and working classes. In 1912, the Conservatives, finally acknowledging the demand for change, introduced the secret ballot and granted all adult males the right to vote.

In 1916, the UCR leader Hipólito Irigoyen was elected president. Despite retaining the presidency for fourteen years, he could not break the power of the ruling classes. Economic problems caused by the Depression in 1930 prompted a military coup d'état. Argentina suffered under a harsh regime of repression and corruption for thirteen years after this uprising. Supported by the military, the Conservatives rigged the ballots to ensure they retained power.

In 1943, with militant unions and a disgruntled middle class threatening rebellion, the military staged another coup. A key figure in the subsequent government was Colonel Juan Perón. As Minister of Labor, he defied the Conservatives to reform labor laws, increase wages, and encourage trade unions to expand.

In 1946, backed by the General Labor Confederation (CGT), Perón won the presidency as the candidate of the Argentine Labor Party's candidate. He was ably supported by his glamorous wife Eva (Evita). Despite their flamboyant lifestyle, the Perons cleverly retained the support of the labor movement.

In 1951, Perón won a second term as leader of the Perónist Party. He became an authoritarian leader, crushing strikes and slashing workers' wages in an attempt to revitalize the flagging economy. By 1955 the country had grown dissatisfied with Perón. When the Catholic Church withdrew its support, the military staged a coup d'état, removing him from office.

Thus began eighteen years of repressive and violent military rule. Inflation rose dramatically and the country was wracked by industrial disputes and high unemployment. Congress was closed down in 1966 and all political parties banned.

The hard-line military leaders reluctantly allowed the Perónist Party to contest the 1973 presidential election. Héctor Cámpora, the party's successful candidate, resigned shortly after his election. This paved the way for Juan Perón's return to power. When he died the following year his place was taken by his third wife, Isabel.

Neither was able to stabilize the country. A general strike and increasing activity by guerilla movements prompted the military to take control again in March of 1976. A new and hor-

The harbor of Ushuaia, Tierra del Fuego, in the far south of Argentina.

Argentina

rific period of torture, murder, abduction and repression ensued. A succession of military leaders led to the appointment of General Leopoldo Galtieri as president in 1981.

To divert attention from the military's appalling record, Galtieri staged an invasion of the Falkland Islands in 1982. The islands, a British possession in the south Atlantic Ocean, were known to Argentinians as Las Malvinas. Britain's control had long been disputed by Argentina. Argentinian forces surrendered to Britain after a short encounter.

Discredited and humiliated, the military government collapsed. Elections were held in 1983 for a civilian government. The Radical Civic Union, after defeating the Perónist Party, faced huge problems. The economy was weak, inflation was growing, and military unrest threatened rebellion.

The Perónist Party, led by Carlos Menem, regained power in 1989. Menem followed an International Monetary Fund (IMF) program which required severe cuts in social expenditure. Linking the peso to the U. S. dollar to stabilize the Argentine currency made matters worse. Some people did well during this period, but most Argentinians faced hardship.

The Alianza party came to power in 1999, with Fernando de la Rúa as president. De la Rúa attempted to improve the economy with tax increases and spending cuts. The economy did not respond, forcing Argentina to again go to the IMF in late 2000 for a U.S.$40 million aid package. By the end of the following year, the IMF demanded that additional cuts be made. This led to violent protests in which more than 25 people were killed. De la Rúa resigned in December, 2001.

The Congress appointed Eduardo Duhalde of the Justicialist Party as president in 2002. After suspending payment on a massive foreign debt, the government decided to end the link between the peso and the U.S. dollar. The currency plunged dramatically in value, throwing the country into even greater crisis. Banks closed their doors and people were cut off from access to their savings. Subsequent political instability has meant a gloomy outlook for the country that was once the most prosperous in South America.

The spectacular Iguaza Falls on Argentina's border with Brazil.

Armenia

REPUBLIC OF ARMENIA

GOVERNMENT
Website www.gov.am
Capital
Yerevan
Type of government Republic
Voting Universal adult suffrage
Head of state
President
Head of government
Prime Minister
Constitution 1995
Legislature
Unicameral National Assembly
Judiciary Supreme Court
Member of
CE, IMF, UN, UNESCO, WHO

LAND AND PEOPLE
Land area
11,500 sq mi (29,000 sq km)
Highest point
Aragats Lerrnagagat
13,252 ft (4090 m)
Population
3,330,000
Major cities and populations
Yerevan 1.4 million
Ethnic groups
Armenian 92%, Others 8%
Religions
Christianity 99%
Languages
Armenian (official)

ECONOMIC
Currency dram
Industry
machinery, tires, clothing, footwear,
chemicals, motor vehicles,
electronics, jewellery, computer
software, food processing
Agriculture
fruit, vegetables, livestock
Natural resources
gold, copper, molybdenum, zinc

Rugged mountains and deep gorges make up most of Armenia, a tiny, landlocked country bordering Georgia, Azerbaijan, Turkey and Iran. The average height of the country's land is 5,000 feet (1,500 m), while the highest mountain exceeds 13,000 feet (4000 m). Winters in Armenia are very cold, and its summers very hot and dry. The country gets little rain, so periods of serious drought often occur.

More than ninety percent of the people are ethnic Armenians. The others are Azeri, Russians and Kurds. Most residents belong to the Armenian Orthodox Church, yet there are some Protestants and a small group of Muslims. Armenian is the official language. In the past, manufacturing, mining, and agriculture have employed many Armenians. At the present time, the breakup of the Soviet Union and ongoing conflict with Aberbaijan have greatly affected the economy.

Indigenous peoples formed the kingdom of Urartu during the eighth century B.C. After Persia conquered Urartu in the sixth century, the region was given its present name. Persian rule fell to the Greeks in the fourth century. The Greeks were displaced by the Romans in 69 B.C. Persia regained control in the third century A.D., followed by Arabs, the Byzantine Empire, and Mongols.

The Turkish Ottoman Empire had seized power by the sixteenth century. At times, Armenia flourished under Ottoman control. However, as the time passed, oppression of the Armenians increased. In the late nineteenth century, fearing Armenian loyalty to Russia, the Ottomans killed hundreds of thousands of them. During World War I, as Armenia became a battleground, nearly a million more died.

Russia prevailed after World War I. Armenia, Azerbaijan, and Georgia became the Transcaucasian Soviet Federated Socialist Republic. In 1936, Armenia became a separate Soviet republic. When the Soviet Union ended, Armenian declared its independence in August of 1991.

Most of Nagorno-Karabakh, a region in Azerbaijan, is an ethnic Armenian enclave. Fighting began when Armenians demanded that Azerbaijan give them this land. A cease-fire was declared, with Russian assistance, in 1994. U.S. Secretary of State Colin Powell led peace talks between Armenia and Azerbaijan in 2001. The question of control of the Nagorno-Karabakh region has yet to be resolved.

Gunmen entered the Armenian parliament building in October of 1999. The prime minister and seven other government officials were assassinated.

Australia

COMMONWEALTH OF AUSTRALIA

Australia is a country as well as the world's smallest continent. It is located in the southern hemisphere, about 2,000 miles (3,2000 km) southeast of mainland Asia and about 7,000 miles (11,000 km) southwest of North America. The landscape is relatively flat, with an average elevation of 900 feet (275 m). Arid desert in the central regions makes up about half the continent. Coastal plains running from the far northeast around to the south and southwest are highly fertile. Forests occupy just under twenty percent of the land. Tasmania, an island off the coast of mainland Australia, is a part of the continent and country.

The climate of Australia varies a good deal throughout the country. Southern regions experience cold winters and warm to hot summers. In the north it is almost always warm to hot, with high humidity, particularly in January and February. Rainfall varies enormously. The coastal areas receive regular and plentiful rain, unlike the interior region. Droughts are common in this area, with some places receiving no rain for years at a time.

Indigenous peoples total slightly more than one percent of the population. Most of them live in northern and central regions across Queensland, the Northern Territory, and Western Australia. The majority of the population are immigrants or the descendants of immigrants. A large number have British and Irish backgrounds, while smaller groups are of Italian, Greek, Southeast Asian, and Eastern European descent. There was large-scale refugee immigration from the Middle East and Vietnam in the 1970s. Chinese immigrants began arriving during the 1850s gold rushes. Under the White Australia Policy, which lasted from 1901 to 1967, only selected Europeans were admitted as migrants.

Religious freedom is guaranteed under the 1900 constitution. Most people have Christian backgrounds. The major denominations are the Catholic, Anglican and Uniting churches, with other Christian denominations widely represented. Buddhism and Islam each account for around one percent of the population and there is also a small Jewish community. Close to twenty percent of all Australians claim to have no religious faith.

The official language is English. It is not uncommon for native languages to be spoken within some immigrant groups. Indigenous Australians are known to have spoken up to 260 different languages.

Over two-thirds of Australians earn their living in the service industry. Banks, hospitals, stores, restaurants, and government agencies employ

SCOTT BRODIE

This land, originally cleared for farming, has been severely affected by salination.

large numbers of people. The need for workers in hotels, restaurants, transportation, and communication has grown with Australia's tourism industry.

Since the 1980s, lower air fares have brought large numbers of visitors from North America, Europe and particularly Asia. Eager tourists come to see Australia's prosperous cities, wildlife sanctuaries, beautiful beaches, and the famous Great Barrier Reef. Since the highly successful 2000 Olympics in Sydney, tourism continues to soar at an even higher rate. Large sums of money have been spent developing resorts across the country, as well as for building new airports and roads.

Vast areas of the coastal plains are dedicated to growing crops and raising livestock for domestic needs and export. Wheat is the predominant export crop, followed by fruits, sugar cane, rice, and cotton. Poppies, cultivated in Tasmania, supply world markets with legal opium for medical use. In many areas, large-scale irrigation is used, particularly in the cultivation of rice and cotton.

The rich plains provide important grazing pastures for sheep and cattle. The dairy industry supplies local and Asian markets. Australia is the world's largest beef exporter, supplying much of the hamburger meat sold in the United

States. Australia produces 25% of the wool used throughout the world.

Manufacturing is concentrated in the southeastern region. Products include motor vehicles, electrical goods, textiles, processed foods, chemicals, and telecommunications equipment.

Australia supplies much of the coal and iron ore used by Japanese and Korean heavy industry. Black coal is mined along much of the east coast. Open-cut iron ore mines are found in the northwest. Bass Strait, between the mainland and Tasmania, is the nation's primary source of oil. Extensive natural gas deposits are found in the north of South Australia and off the northwest coast. There are also substantial reserves of lead, bauxite, uranium, diamonds, gold, silver and zinc.

Australia is a federal parliamentary state, made up of six states, two territories and several external territories. The parliamentary system is modelled on England's government, with refinements from the American system. The Queen of England, as head of state, is represented by the governor-general, who is selected by the government.

The cabinet, led by the prime minister, forms the government and holds office with the support of the House of

GOVERNMENT
Website www.gov.au
Capital Canberra
Type of government
Federal parliamentary state
Independence from Britain
January 1, 1901 (dominion status)
Voting
Universal adult suffrage, compulsory
Head of state British Crown,
represented by Governor-General
Head of government Prime Minister
Constitution 1901
Legislature
Bicameral Parliament
House of Representatives (lower house),
Senate (upper house)
Judiciary High Court
Member of
APEC, CN, IMF, OECD, SPF, UN,
UNESCO, UNHCR, WHO, WTO

LAND AND PEOPLE
Land area 2,966,141 sq mi
(7,682,300 sq km)
Highest point
Mount Kosciusko 7,310 ft (2368 m)
Coastline 16,000 mi (25,760 km)
Population 19,808,205
Major cities and populations
Sydney 3.9 million
Melbourne 3.3 million
Brisbane 1.5 million
Perth 1.3 million
Adelaide 1 million
Canberra 0.3 million
Ethnic groups European 90%, Asian
7%, indigenous 1%, others 2%
Religions Christianity 80%, others 20%
Languages
English (official), indigenous languages

ECONOMIC
Currency Australian dollar
Industry
tourism, mining, agriculture, motor
vehicles, steel, food processing, chemicals
Agriculture
wheat, barley, sugar cane, fruits, beef
cattle, sheep, wool, poultry, dairy
Natural resources
bauxite, coal, copper, iron ore, tin, silver,
uranium, nickel, tungsten, lead, zinc,
diamonds, natural gas, petroleum

Australia

The Twelve Apostles — large rock formations in southeastern Australia.

Captain James Cook of Britain's Royal Navy first sighted the eastern coastline in 1770. He had been sent to learn more about the large continent in the southern hemisphere. His first landing was at Botany Bay, close to the present-day Sydney. Reaching the far north of the coast, Cook took possession for Britain, naming it New South Wales.

Over the next ten years rumors persisted that France planned to claim at least part of the continent. Joseph Banks, the eminent scientist who accompanied Cook, was eager to see it become a British colony.

After the American Revolution, England was no longer free to send its convicted criminals

Representatives. The parliament is bicameral. Members of the House of Representatives, the lower house, are elected for three year terms. Members of the Senate, or upper house, serve six-year terms. The states and territories have their own governments, which operate similarly to the national government.

For at least 60,000 years before the arrival of Europeans, the continent was occupied by indigenous peoples, known collectively as Aborigines. It is believed they migrated south across a land bridge which then joined Australia to Asia. Once this link was broken, their civilizations developed in isolation until the coming of the Europeans. Written records are very limited, so a full history is difficult to relate.

Spanish and Portuguese navigators first sighted the western coast in the early 1600s. They found little of interest. Dutch explorers of the mid-1600s, who called the region New Holland, made no attempts at settlement. William Dampier, an English sailor, landed on the northwest coast in 1688. The uncharted continent was vaguely marked on maps as 'Terra Australis' or South Land.

Sheep farming is one of Australia's major industries.

to the American colonies. Chronic overcrowding in British jails led Banks to suggest Botany Bay as an ideal location for a penal colony.

On January 26, 1788, eleven ships loaded with convicts and supplies arrived at Port Jackson (Sydney Harbor) to establish the new colony. Conditions were harsh. The new arrivals faced starvation for several years before supplies arrived and wheat was successfully cultivated. Aboriginal peoples who lived in the region were gradually driven from their lands, despite fierce resistance.

A second penal colony was established on Van Diemen's Land in the early 1800s. It was later renamed Tasmania. It was for the very worst offenders and soon gained a reputation as a place of great hardship and cruelty.

The New South Wales Corps, formed to guard the convicts, quickly became corrupted. Its officers set up businesses importing goods, especially rum. These activities led to constant friction with governors. Corruption reached its peak in 1808 when the Corps deposed Governor William Bligh (of HMS Bounty fame). In 1810 Colonel Lachlan Macquarie arrived to replace Bligh.

The Sydney Harbor Bridge and Sydney Opera House are at the heart of the nation's largest city.

SCOTT BRODIE

Australia

Sub-tropical Brisbane is Australia's third-largest city.

Sub-tropical Brisbane is Australia's third-largest city.

SCOTT BRODIE

Macquarie's Black Watch Regiment replaced the old Corps.

During Macquarie's term, from 1810 to 1821, New South Wales was transformed from a squalid convict settlement into a growing and prosperous colony. Immigration by free settlers increased dramatically. Under increasing pressure from the free settlers, Britain ended transportation of convicts to New South Wales and Van Diemen's Land in the 1840s.

Immigrants poured into the colonies in the 1850s following discovery of fabulous gold deposits. Thousands flocked from Britain, China and the United States. Melbourne was one of the wealthiest cities in the British Empire within a decade.

By the 1890s there were six colonies: New South Wales, Tasmania, Victoria, Queensland, South Australia and Western Australia. Following several inter-colonial conventions, a federation of states was created. The British parliament passed legislation in 1900 which federated the six colonies under a national government. The Commonwealth of Australia, a British domin-

ion, was established on January 1, 1901.

The infamous White Australia Policy was introduced in 1901. Its aim was to expel Chinese immigrants and stop immigration by anyone who was not a white European. It remained in place until the 1960s when social attitudes forced a change. Since then, immigration has been opened to people of all nations.

In World War I, Australian troops fought for Britain in Turkey, the Middle East, and France. When World War II broke out in 1939, Australian troops were sent to the Middle East and northern Africa. Thousands were captured by

the Japanese in Singapore and Malaysia. In 1942, Australian troops stopped the Japanese advance in the jungles of Papua New Guinea. Australia was used as the command base for Allied forces under the command of U.S. General Douglas MacArthur.

After the war, a new Labor government introduced widespread social reforms. It also began the largest immigration program in the nation's history, welcoming hundreds of thousands from the war-devastated countries of Europe. After the war, these people worked tirelessly on various national development projects.

Australia increasingly allied itself with the United States, seeking to stem the advance of communism in Asia. Air, naval and ground units joined the United Nations forces in the Korean War. They also joined forces with Britain in the Malayan Emergency and with the United States in the Vietnam War.

For sixteen years, beginning in 1950, the nation was governed by Liberal Party prime minister Robert Menzies. It was a time of great prosperity, largely due to huge profits from wool and wheat exports. High import tariffs caused local industries to thrive.

Twenty-three years of conservative rule ended when a Labor government led by Gough Whitlam was elected in 1972. Far-reaching social and economic changes had a profound effect on Australian society. However, amid pressure from states' groups, the Whitlam government was dismissed by the governor-general in 1975.

Australia shifted its attention from Europe to Asia during the 1980s and 1990s. Prime Minister Paul Keating (1991–96) was an enthusiastic proponent of closer economic and cultural relations with the nations of Southeast Asia. Since that time, closer ties have evolved with both Thailand and Singapore.

The return of land to indigenous peoples began in the mid-1970s. It accelerated a good deal in the 1990s when High Court judgments favored the indigenous peoples. Reconciliation of indigenous and immigrant Australians continues.

Although independent, Australia has the British monarch as its head of state. A growing movement for a change to a republic led to a referendum during 1999. The government of Prime Minister John Howard (1996 -) refused to support it and people could not agree on the method of choosing a head of state, so the measure failed to win passage.

The government came under increasing international criticism over its policy of imprisoning refugees and asylum seekers in 2000. Iraqi and Afghan refugees have been placed in desert internment camps with limited communication with the outside.

A group of asylum seekers were rescued from a sinking boat by a container ship off northwestern Australia in late 2001. The government seized the ship to block it from reaching Australia. It then paid governments in Papua New Guinea and Nauru to hold the arrivals in internment camps, to prevent them from landing on Australian soil.

Asylum seekers in an Australian internment camp awaiting permission to stay or to be returned to their country

NEWSPIX

Austria

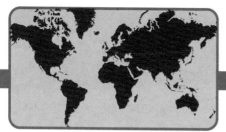

REPUBLIC OF AUSTRIA

Landlocked Austria is located in central Europe. The European Alps dominate the landscape, occupying seventy-five percent of the country. The highest point is the Grossglockner peak at 12,457 feet (3797 m). In the north-west, the Granite Plateau forms an upland region stretching into the Czech Republic. The highly fertile lowlands of the east make ideal agricultural land. The river system is dominated by the Danube into which most other streams empty. More than forty percent of the land is covered by forests.

Austria's climate varies according to the altitude. Higher regions are alpine and can be extremely cold throughout the year. There are heavy snowfalls during winter. Lower areas are continental, enjoying a relatively pleasant climate with cool to cold winters and warm summers.

The people are overwhelmingly of Germanic origin. Almost sixty percent live in densely populated urban areas. Situated on the border of a number of eastern European countries, Austria has seen a vast number of refugees cross its borders since 1945. About eighty percent of the people are Christian and the majority of those are Catholics. Austria is also home to a large minority of Jewish and Muslim people. German is the national language. Various small minorities speak Eastern European languages.

Austria is self-sufficient in food production, much of which takes place on small farms. Potatoes, fruit, beet sugar, oats, and barley are key crops. In mountain regions there is a thriving dairy industry. Mineral extraction is also important to

The stunning Schoenbrun Palace, from the heyday of the Habsburg dynasty.

SCOTT BRODIE

the nation's economy. Graphite, magnesium, iron ore, copper, zinc, and lignite are all mined in many areas.

Manufacturing contributes substantially to the economy. Most industries are located in Vienna or its surrounding regions. They are assisted by a plentiful supply of energy from hydroelectric facilities. The major products are motor vehicles, chemicals, textiles, paper, steel, electrical goods and processed foods.

Services now employ more than fifty percent of the Austrian workforce. Banking and associated services are a key part of the service industry sector. Austria's long history and spectacular landscape make tourism a significant contributor to the national economy.

Austria is a republic. The head of state is the president who is elected to a six-year term by a vote of the people. There is a bicameral parliament. Members of the lower house, or Nationalrat, are elected by the people. The upper house, known as the Bundesrat, consists of members nominated by the provincial assemblies. The prime minister, or chancellor, and Cabinet run the government. The chancellor is named by the president, while both leaders decide on the members of the Cabinet. The Nationalrat members have the right to approve or oppose

the policies of the chancellor and the Cabinet.

The region of Austria was populated by Celts until the first century B.C. Following invasion by the Romans, it was divided into a number of provinces. The area prospered under Roman influence. The fifth century A.D. saw invasions by Asiatic and Germanic tribes. These included the Huns, Ostrogoths, Lombards and Barbarians. Most of the provinces were destroyed in their rampages.

Charlemagne, king of the Franks, invaded Austria in 788. Shortly thereafter, he was crowned Holy Roman Emperor. Christianity, first introduced at this time, was encouraged and spread widely. However, when Charlemagne died in 814, the Frankish empire was split up, and Austria was conquered by the Magyars.

The area was seized by Emperor Otto II in 955. After being made Holy Roman Emperor, Otto II handed Austria to Leopold of Babenberg in 976. The Babenberg family ruled the region for the next 270 years. They made Vienna their capital in 1142. The last of the Babenberg line died in battle in 1246.

A period of bloody warfare followed, from which Austria emerged as a territory of King Rudolf of Habsburg. The Habsburgs had a huge impact on

GOVERNMENT
Website www.austria.gv.at
Capital Vienna
Type of government Republic
Voting Universal adult suffrage
Head of state President
Head of government Chancellor
Constitution 1920
Legislature
Bicameral Federal Assembly
(Bundesversammlung)
Federal Council (Bundesrat)
National Council (Nationalrat)
Judiciary Supreme Judicial Court
Member of
CE, EU, IMF, OECD, UN, UNESCO,
UNHCR, WHO, WTO

LAND AND PEOPLE
Land area 32,378 sq mi (83,858 sq km)
Highest point Grossglockner 3798 m
Population 8,169,929
Major cities and populations
Vienna 1,600,000
Graz 240,000
Linz 200,000
Ethnic groups
Austrian 96%, others 4%
Religions
Christianity 86%, others 8%
Language German

ECONOMIC
Currency Euro
Industry
machinery, motor vehicles, food,
chemicals, timber products,
paper products, communications
equipment, tourism
Agriculture
grains, potatoes, beet sugar,
wine, fruit; dairy, cattle, pigs,
poultry, timber
Natural resources
iron ore, oil, timber, magnesite,
lead, coal, lignite, copper

Austria

The majestic alpine landscape at Innsbruck.

Austrian history. They spent the next three hundred years assembling a major empire in central Europe. They gained-control of Spain. A determined siege of Vienna in 1529 was repelled by Habsburg armies.

Devout Catholics, the Habsburgs vigorously opposed the Protestant Reformation movement begun in Germany by Martin Luther. Their stance led to the Thirty Years' War from 1618 to 1648. Austria and Spain, both Catholic, went to war against Protestant England, Germany, Denmark, the Netherlands, and Sweden. The outcome specified that a nation's leader could choose the religion of his subjects.

Charles VI, the last male member of the Habsburg dynasty, died in 1740. He had directed that all his lands pass to his daughter Maria Theresa. France, Spain and Bavaria challenged this ruling. This began the 1740–48 War of Succession. Austria won the battle, with the aid of Britain and the Netherlands. Maria Theresa's husband became emperor.

Maria Theresa, and subsequently her son Joseph, set about reforming Austria's social structure. The old feudal system was abolished and a central administration created. Freedom of religion was guaranteed and the arts were encouraged. The golden age of music, for which Austria is famous, began at this time.

The peace was violently interrupted by Napoleon Bonaparte's French armies, which invaded Austria in 1797. The military campaigns ended in the 1805 Battle of Austerlitz, which was disastrous for Austria. Napoleon placed Austria in a regional grouping called the Confederation of the Rhine. There were several more military defeats before the invaders could be expelled.

Austria joined the successful campaign against Napoleon in 1813. Following his defeat, the Congress of Vienna was held in 1814–15. Austria's reward was an expansion of its territory into several parts of northern Italy. Guided by the master politician Clemems Metternich, Austria became the leading member of the German Confederation. When peace resumed there was another great flowering of literature and music, notably in Vienna.

The mid-nineteenth century saw a wave of democratic change sweep Europe. In Austria a number of rebellions broke out in 1848. After some initial successes, they were suppressed. Enthusiasm for change spread to Hungary, which was under Austria's control. This led to dissent over

Some of the spectacular architecture that makes Vienna unique.

the Austrian leadership of the German Confederation. Emperor Ferdinand abdicated in favor of his nephew Franz Joseph.

Austria then began declining as a major European power. Its demise was hastened by defeat in the Austro-Prussian War of 1866. The German territories came under the control of Prussia, led by Otto von Bismarck. Austrian control over Hungary was stabilized the following year when the Austrian emperor became the Hungarian king as well.

The final years of this Austro-Hungarian Empire saw a great flowering of social and

SCOTT BRODIE

cultural life. There was also substantial economic growth. Austria led the way for much of Europe by granting universal adult suffrage in 1907.

In the early years of the twentieth century, the empire faced incessant demands for independence from its Slav subjects in the Balkans. Austria-Hungary had expanded its borders by annexing Bosnia and Herzegovina in 1908. Russia supported the Slav nationalists, leading Austria into an alliance with the German Empire.

All of this came to a head in June, 1914, when a Serbian assassinated Archduke Ferdinand at Sarajevo. Ferdinand was the heir to the Austrian throne and Austria-Hungary responded by threatening war with independent Serbia. Russia mobilized its forces in support of Serbia. Germany backed Austria-Hungary. Other European nations lined up with Russia and World War I broke out a short time later.

The war, which lasted from 1914 to 1918, was a horrendous bloodbath. Millions died in futile attempts to win territory, particularly in France and Belgium. Germany's defeat in 1918 led to the collapse of the Austro-Hungarian Empire. Emperor Franz Joseph died in 1916. He was succeeded by his great-nephew Charles. After the crushing defeat, Charles abdicated in November of 1918. This

Austria

Street life in Vienna, Austria's capital.

enabled the formation of the Republic of Austria. Karl Renner was the first chancellor of the new nation. Post-war treaties broke up the Austro-Hungarian Empire. Austria was reduced to the area it occupies today.

In the past, Austria had been structured to function as the center of an empire. However, alliances with Germany or other countries were now forbidden. With food and raw materials in short supply, the economy collapsed. People starved while inflation surged out of control. Austria did gain some relief from a League of Nations aid package.

The high unemployment and ongoing financial crises led to political unrest. Vienna's socialist government was increasingly at odds with conservatives in rural areas. Each side formed private armies, creating further instability.

As it had in Germany, National Socialism rose to popularity in the early 1930s. Socialism opponent Engelbert Dolfuss, who became chancellor in 1932, was assassinated by Nazis in 1934. His successor, Kurt von Schuschnigg, was forced out of office by Germany in 1938. This opened the way for the Anschluss, the annexation of Austria by German troops. It was now part of Germany's Third Reich.

When World War II ended in 1945, Austria was occupied by the victorious Allies. The United States, Britain, France and the Soviet Union shared control of the country. Reconstruction and economic aid was delivered by the United States under its Marshall Plan in the late 1940s. Following lengthy negotiations, the occupying powers withdrew in 1955. Austria again became a nation in its own right.

Post-war Austrian politicians were determined to avoid the turmoil of the 1930s. The country was ruled by a coalition of political parties until 1966. This stable arrangement led to extensive economic and social advancement. In June 1994 Austrians voted overwhelmingly in favor of joining the European Union.

Austria has had to cope with refugees from the neighboring Balkans. It accepted more than 80,000 people fleeing the war in Bosnia. While most Austrians have strongly supported such humanitarian programs, there has been growing opposition in the late 1990s. The rise of right-wing nationalists under Joerg Haider is evidence of this. Haider was forced to resign from a coalition government in 2000, following diplomatic sanctions by other European nations.

Azerbaijan

REPUBLIC OF AZERBAIJAN

Located in central Asia, Azerbaijan is bordered by Iran, Armenia, Georgia, and Russia, and the Caspian Sea.

A small part of the country, called Nakhichevan, lies within Armenia's borders. About half of the landscape is made up of the Caucasus Mountains, while most of the rest is low-lying plains. The climate varies a good deal, with freezing temperatures in winter and highs of up to 35°C in summer.

Ninety percent of the people are ethnic Azeris. The majority of the population is Shi'ite Muslim. The official language is Azerbaijani. The language was written in the Cyrillic (Russian) alphabet until 1992, when Latin script was adopted.

Petroleum, natural gas, and metals industries employ about half of the workers in Azerbaijan. A large percentage of the others are in farming.

Profits from oil reserves beneath the Caspian Sea dominate the Azerbaijani economy. International oil producers signed agreements to invest U.S. $30 billion in drilling and pipeline construction during the 1990s.

Azerbaijan was controlled by the Medes in the eighth century B.C. It fell to the Persians in the sixth century B.C. Arabs conquered the region in the late seventh century A.D., bringing Islam to its people. During the next many years, the area was controlled by Mongols, Turks, and Persians.

Persian rule fell to Russia in the early 1800s. During this time, Azerbaijan developed a prosperous petroleum industry.

Following the 1917 Russian Revolution, Azerbaijan declared its independence. However, it was conquered by the Soviet Red Army in 1920. It became part of the Transcaucasian Soviet Federal Socialist Republic. Azerbaijan joined the Soviet Union in 1936.

The Popular Front of Azerbaijan (PFA) led rebellions in 1989–90. Soviet troops were brought in to suppress the independence movement. Azerbaijan formally broke from the Soviet Union in September of 1991 and elected its first non-communist president in seventy years. Azerbaijan became a member of the Commonwealth of Independent States (CIS) in 1993.

Within Azerbaijan's borders, an area called Nagorno-Karabakh has an Armenian majority. Russia had given this area to Azerbaijan in 1923. Armenia's claim to this land began a bitter war in 1992. More than 15,000 people were killed and about one million were left homeless as a result of the fighting. A cease-fire was declared in 1994. The U.S. led peace talks in 2001. Control of the Nagorno-Krabakh region has yet to be resolved.

The Bahamas

COMMONWEALTH OF THE BAHAMAS

The Bahamas is a chain of over 3000 coral islands and reefs southeast of Florida and north of Cuba. About eighty percent of Bahamians live on the islands of New Providence and Grand Bahama. The climate is subtropical and generally very pleasant. Beautiful beaches and crystal clear waters attract over three million people annually.

Most of the population is descended from African slaves who arrived in the eighteenth century. The rest are of mixed African-European or British background. The Bahamas is overwhelmingly Christian and English is the official language. Nearly one hundred percent of Bahamians can read and write.

Lucayans, a branch of the Arawak peoples, were the original inhabitants. Christopher Columbus landed in the Bahamas in 1492. He claimed the islands for Spain. In subsequent visits, Spaniards captured and enslaved the Lucayans, taking them off to Hispaniola.

The islands were a stronghold of pirates for many years. The British settled Eleuthra and New Providence in 1648. The pirates were eliminated. An American revolutionary force briefly held the Bahamas in 1776. Spain seized control in 1781.

Britain regained the Bahamas under the Treaty of Paris in 1783. United States'

farmers brought large numbers of African slaves to work on cotton plantations. Britain abolished slavery in 1834. The economy declined and many people left the islands. A serious cholera epidemic in the mid 1800s further decreased the population.

The Bahamas became a Union base during the American Civil War. U.S. liquor smugglers of the 1920s used the islands as well. During World War II, the Bahamas were bases for the U.S. military.

Full internal self-government was granted to the colony in 1964. Three years later, the predominantly European government was toppled by the Progressive Liberal Party (PLP). The country became independent on July 10, 1973. PLP leader Lynden Pindling became prime minister. He held office until 1992, amid charges of corruption. The Free National Movement prevailed until 2002, when PLP candidate Perry Christie took office.

Tourism, the major growth industry since the 1950s, employs nearly half the people. The islands are visited by over three million people each year.

Due to favorable tax laws, many Bahamians work in the thriving financial services industry. Unfortunately, allegations of large-scale drug trafficking on the islands continue.

GOVERNMENT
Website www.bahamas.gov.bs
Capital Nassau
Type of government
Independent commonwealth
Independence from Britain
July 10, 1973
Voting Universal adult suffrage
Head of state
British Crown,
represented by Governor-General
Head of government
Prime Minister
Constitution 1973
Legislature
Bicameral parliament
House of Assembly (lower house),
Senate (upper house)
Judiciary Supreme Court
Member of
Caricom, CN, IMF, OAS, UN,
UNESCO, WHO

LAND AND PEOPLE
Land area 5,382 sq mi
(13,939 sq km)
Highest point
Mount Alvernia 204 ft (63 m)
Coastline 2,200 mi (3,542 km)
Population 300,529
Major cities and populations
Nassau 195,000
Ethnic groups
African 75%, African-European
15%, European 10%
Religion Christianity
Languages English (official),
English creole, French creole

ECONOMIC
Currency Bahamian dollar
Industry
tourism, banking, cement, oil
refining and shipment, salt, rum,
aragonite, pharmaceuticals, steel
piping
Agriculture
citrus, vegetables, poultry
Natural resources
salt, aragonite, timber

Bahrain

STATE OF BAHRAIN

The State of Bahrain is off the eastern coast of Saudi Arabia. It is made up of a large island and more than thirty smaller islands in the Persian Gulf. Most of the islands are desert with extreme heat and little rainfall. Natural springs in northern areas of the large island provide water for people and plant life.

Around 65 percent of the people are Bahrain Arabs. Most of the others are Iranians, as well as other Arabs and Asians. Islam is the state religion, practiced by about 85 percent of the people, who are either Shi'ite or Sunni Muslims. Arabic is the official language, yet English is widely spoken in business.

About five thousand years ago, Bahrain was a trading civilization known as Dilmun. Persia ruled the region, beginning in the fourth century A.D. Nestorian Christianity was introduced. The Abbasids took power in the 700s, bringing Islam to the country. Brief rule by the Portuguese in the 1500s was followed by a return of the Persians. Members of the Bani Utub tribe from Qatar founded the Al-Khalifa dynasty in 1783.

For many years, Great Britain helped defend the country against invaders from Saudi Arabia. The Al-Khalifa to accepted a number of treaties, which made Bahrain a British protectorate in 1861. It later became known as one of the Trucial States.

During the early 1900s, the nation worked to develop better programs and facilities for its people. In 1932, its petroleum industry began. This significantly altered the country's economy. Agitation against British control brought independence in 1971.

A parliamentary government held the first national elections in 1973, under head of state Emir Isa bin Sulman al-Khalifa. Within a few years, the emir dissolved the legislature and ended voting, giving himself absolute control. In 1999, successor Sheik Hamad bin Isa al-Khalifa, promoted change to a constitutional monarchy, with a legislature and voting rights for all adults.

The country has been in a dispute with Qatar over control of the Hawar Islands and the natural-gas-rich Dome region. The International Court of Justice awarded the islands to Bahrain in 2001.

Financial services remain a viable part of Bahrain's economy. The country is working to strengthen its position as an international banking center.

The United States Navy's Fifth Fleet is based in Bahrain. During the 1991 Persian Gulf War and in the 2003 war against Saddam Hussein, Bahrain provided valuable cooperation to coalition forces.

Bangladesh

FLAT EARTH PICTURE GALLERY

Children in the waters of the great river delta that dominates Bangladesh.

The Asian nation of Bangladesh lies on the Bay of Bengal, to the west of Burma, south and east of India. The northern region lies in the foothills of the Himalayas. Its most prominent natural feature is the vast delta in the south where the great Ganges, Brahmaputra and Meghna Rivers converge. This makes the land very fertile, but also creates terrible flooding. Bangladesh has a tropical monsoon climate. June to October is the wet season with heavy rainfall, high humidity, and high temperatures. There are also occasional devastating cyclones.

More than 130 million people live in the nation's 56,000 square miles (134,000 sq km). All but two percent of the population is Bengali. The rest are Bihari or from hill tribes in the Chittagong region. Islam is the state religion. Most people are Sunni Muslims, while a much smaller number are Hindus. There are tiny Christian and Buddhist minorities. Bangla (or Bengali) is the official language, with English commonly used for business. About 100 tribal dialects are still spoken.

A very poor country, Bangladesh relies heavily on foreign aid. Agriculture dominates the economy. Secondary industry is of only minor importance. Sugar cane, jute, tea, rice and wheat are the major crops. Processed foods, jute products, textiles, steel and fertilizers are the main secondary industries. Despite the fertility of the land, Bangladesh imports large quantities of food to feed its population.

Bangladesh was originally part of the region known as Bengal. It was controlled from Delhi in India until 1341. It then had various Muslim rulers before the Mughal emperor Akbar invaded in 1576. The eighteenth century saw the British East India Company exerting control over the region. Bengal became a primary source of opium which the British traded to China in the 1800s.

Independence came in 1947. India was partitioned into two dominions, India and Pakistan. The first was predominantly Hindu, the second predominantly Muslim. What is now Bangladesh was called East Pakistan. On the other side of India was West Pakistan, where the nation's leadership was based.

The people of the east grew increasingly resentful about the political power of the west. They believed all the economic benefits were going to West Pakistan. Martial law was declared in 1958. Violent uprising had grown from unrest in the divided nation. The desire for autonomy strengthened the pro-independence Awami League. It gained most of East Pakistan's seats in the national parliament. Parliament was suspended and the League's leader was imprisoned.

East Pakistan, renamed Bangladesh, declared independence on March 26, 1971. When an army, composed entirely of soldiers from West Pakistan, occupied the country, civil war erupted. In December, Indian troops entered Bangladesh. Within two weeks they had defeated Pakistan's army. One million Bangladeshis died in the fighting and ten million became refugees to India.

Beginning in 1972, President Sheikh Mujib's government nationalized all major industries, financial institutions and shipping organizations. The time after independence was marked by raging inflation and severe famine. Some months

after Mujib's assassination in 1975, there was a coup d'état by the armed forces. The Bangladesh National Party (BNP) came to power.

During the 1990s there were numerous attempts to stabilize the government and economy, but most ended badly. Accusations of corruption were widespread. In 1996, Hasina Wazed led the opposition Awami League to power. However, the administration was upset in 2001, when the BNP regained control. Efforts to overcome Bangladesh's economic and social problems continue to provoke unrest throughout the country.

The organized chaos of the markets of Dhaka, Bangladesh's capital.

FLAT EARTH PICTURE GALLERY

GOVERNMENT
Website www.bangladeshgov.org
Capital Dhaka
Type of government Republic
Separation from Pakistan
March 26, 1971
Voting Universal adult suffrage
Head of state President
Head of government Prime Minister
Constitution 1972, 1986
Legislature
Unicameral National Parliament (Jatiya Sangsad)
Judiciary Supreme Court
Member of CN, IMF, UN, UNESCO, UNHCR, WHO, WTO

LAND AND PEOPLE
Land area 55,598 sq mi (143,998 sq km)
Highest point Keokradong 4034 ft (1230 m)
Coastline 360 mi (580 km)
Population 133,376,684
Major cities and populations
Dhaka 6.8 million
Chittagong 2.1 million
Khulna 1.2 million
Rajshahi 0.6 million
Ethnic groups
Bengali 98%, other indigenous 2%
Religions
Islam 86%, Hinduism 12%
Languages Bangla (official)

ECONOMIC
Currency Taka
Industry
textiles, jute, garments, tea processing, newsprint, cement, fertilizer, light engineering, sugar
Agriculture
rice, jute, tea, wheat, sugar cane, potatoes, pulses, oilseeds, spices, fruit, beef, dairy, poultry
Natural resources
natural gas, timber, coal

Barbados

One of the Windward Islands in the Caribbean Sea, Barbados has a land area of 166 square miles (431 sq km). Its geography is coral and limestone, with inland terraces rising to 1,104 feet (336 m). The coastal regions are low-lying and fringed by coral reefs. The climate is moderately tropical. Nearly all of the natural vegetation on the island has been cleared for cultivation of farms. Barbados is occasionally subject to hurricanes.

Ninety percent of the people are of African descent. Their ancestors arrived as slaves to work on sugar plantations. The rest are of mixed African-European background. Christianity is the religion of the bulk of the population, but there are small groups of Hindus, Muslims and Jews. English is the official language, but most of the population speaks Barbados' own version of English Creole.

The original residents were Arawak people. It is believed that the Portuguese visited the island in the 1500s. All of the Arawaks had died out by the time of the first British settlement in 1627. Barbados became a crown colony in 1663.

The climate and soils proved ideal for cultivating sugar cane. Plantations were established. Slaves were brought from Africa to work on the plantations. Britain's aboli-tion of slavery in 1834 badly affected the plantations' profits.

Barbados was grouped with Britain's other Windward Islands colonies until it became a separate colony in 1885. In the following decades, the African majority gained strength. Union agitation in the 1930s led to the development of political movements. Chief among these was the Barbados Labour Party (BLP). Limited self-government was granted and universal adult suffrage was introduced in 1950.

Barbados was included in the Federation of the West Indies in 1958. The union proved unworkable. Barbados became independent in its own on November 30, 1966. Labour Party leader Errol Barrow was the first prime minister.

The economy declined during the 1980s. Barbados accepted an International Monetary Fund offer to restructure its finances in 1992.

The country is working to diversity its manufacturing sector, in an effort to reduce its high unemployment rate. Tourism has been aided by the construction of a major marina project at Speightstown. The government is working to encourage more foreign investment. Efforts are being made to reduce a recent upsurge in criminal activity which has affected both tourism and foreign financial interest.

GOVERNMENT
Website www.barbados.gov.bb
Capital Bridgetown
Type of government
Constitutional monarchy
Independence from Britain
November 30, 1966
Voting Universal adult suffrage
Head of state
British Crown,
represented by Governor-General
Head of government Prime Minister
Constitution 1966
Legislature
Bicameral parliament
House of Assembly (lower house)
Senate (upper house)
Judiciary Supreme Court of Judicature
Member of Caricom, CN, IMF, OAS, UN, UNESCO, WHO, WTO

LAND AND PEOPLE
Land area 166 sq mi (431 sq km)
Highest point Mount Hillaby
1,104 ft (336 m)
Coastline 60 mi (97 km)
Population 275,330
Major cities and populations
Bridgetown 133,000
Ethnic groups
African 90%, European 3%, Others 7%
Religion Christianity 99%
Languages
English (official), English Creole

ECONOMIC
Currency Barbadian dollar
Industry
tourism, sugar, light manufacturing, component assembly
Agriculture
sugar cane, vegetables, cotton
Natural resources
petroleum, natural gas, seafood

Belarus

REPUBLIC OF BELARUS

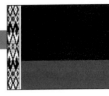

GOVERNMENT
Website www.president.gov.by
Capital Minsk
Type of government Republic
Voting Universal adult suffrage
Head of state President
Head of government
Prime Minister
Constitution 1994
Legislature
Bicameral Parliament
(Natsionalnoye Sobranie)
Chamber of Representatives (Palata
Pretsaviteley), Council of the
Republic (Soviet Respubliki)
Judiciary Supreme Court
Member of
CIS, IMF, UN, UNESCO, WHO

LAND AND PEOPLE
Land area 80,200 sq mi
(207,600 sq km)
Highest point
Dzyarzhynskaya Hara
1,135 ft (346 m)
Population 10,350,194
Major cities and populations
Minsk 1.8 million
Homel 0.6 million
Mahilyou 0.4 million
Ethnic groups
Belarussian 80%, Russian 13%,
Polish 4%, Ukranian 3%
Religion Christianity
Languages Belarussian
(official), Russian

ECONOMIC
Currency Belarussian ruble
Industry
machine tools, tractors, motor
vehicles, earthmoving equipment,
electrical and electronic equipment,
chemicals, fertilizer, textiles
Agriculture
grains, potatoes, vegetables,
beet sugar, flax, dairy, beef
Natural resources
timber, peat, oil, natural gas,
granite, dolomitic limestone,
chalk, clay

Belarus is a landlocked country in northeastern Europe. Most of the landscape is a low-lying plain with small hills. The fertile land is watered by a complex river system. Much of the south is swampland. About one-third o the country is forested. The climate is continental, influenced by the nearby Baltic Sea. Winters are cold, while summers are generally cool to mild.

Seventy percent of the people live in urban areas. Native Belarussians make up almost eighty percent of the population. Most of the rest are Russians, with sizeable Polish and Ukranian minorities. Belarus is overwhelmingly Christian, primarily Eastern Orthodox and Catholic denominations. There are also small Jewish and Muslim groups. Belarussian is the official language.

The Belaur region, populated from prehistoric times, was colonized in the fifth century A.D. by east Slavic tribes. The city-state of Kiev exercised a loose control during the ninth century. Following Kiev's defeat of Mongol invaders, Belaur was formally incorporated into Lithuania in the fourteenth century.

From the sixteenth to the nineteenth century Belarus suffered considerably as a pawn of larger powers. Caught in the middle of wars between Poland and Russia, it gradually came under the latter's control. Poverty in the nineteenth century led many Belarussians to migrate to Asia or North America.

The nation was a battlefield for Russian and German forces in World War I. Belarus proclaimed its independence in March of 1918. The following year, Moscow declared it to be the Belorussian Soviet Socialist Republic. The Red Army was sent in to suppress dissent. After the Russian–Polish War of 1918–20, western Belarus became part of Poland.

Belarus maintained a degree of independence during its years as a Soviet republic. It held its own membership in the United Nations during this time.

Reformers, led by Stanislav Shushkevich, declared complete independence from the Soviet Union on August 25, 1991, Under President Aleksandr Lukashenko, communists took power again in 1994. Lukashenko clashed with parliament over the adoption of a new constitution extending his term.

There has been widespread criticism of human rights abuses in Belarus. Banks, privatized in the early 1990s, have subsequently become re-nationalized. Lukashenko was reelected in 2001. Allegations of election fraud were confronted by intimidation tactics against opponents and the media.

Belgium

KINGDOM OF BELGIUM

Although geographically small, Belgium is one of the most densely populated countries in Europe. It covers an area of 11,787 square miles (30,528 sq km) and is mostly flat, except for the Ardenne Mountains in the south. The central region is very fertile. Twenty percent of the land is covered by forests.

Belgium's temperate climate is heavily influenced by the North Sea in the northwest. Summers are cool to mild. Winters can be very cold in the Ardenne region and cool to cold elsewhere. Summer temperatures range up to 24°C.

There are two distinct cultural regions of Belgium, Wallonia in the south and Flanders in the north. The people of Flanders, called Flemings, speak Dutch. The Walloons of Wallonia speak French. In a smaller area east of Brussels, the people speak German. Christianity is the dominant religion of Belgium.

Belgium is noted for its heavy engineering expertise. Bridges, heavy machinery, surgical equipment, railroad cars, motor vehicles, munitions, and machine tools are all manufactured. A large chemical and petrochemical industry is centered in Antwerp, a city also known as a world leader in the cutting and processing of diamonds. The Liège region concentrates on steel production. The formerly large coal mining sector, in recent decline, is still in operation. Its industrial prosperity has made Belgium one of the wealthiest countries in the world.

The fertile landscape hosts a large and intensive farming industry. Crops such as rye, oats, barley, wheat, sugar beets, flax and potatoes are widely cultivated. Cattle and pigs are also raised and dairy farming is prominent in Flanders. Belgian processed foods are exported around the world. Cheeses and various beverages are at the top of the list of exports.

Belgium is a constitutional monarchy. The hereditary monarch's limited powers include appointing negotiators

The city of Ghent in the East Flanders region.

BRAND X PICTURES

The ancient buildings of Bruges in western Belgium.

who establish a new government following elections. The government is led by a prime minister and a cabinet, all of whom are members of the bicameral legislature. The three main political parties — Liberals, Christian Democrats and Socialists — each have separate Dutch- and French-speaking divisions.

The original inhabitants of the region were fierce Celtic warriors called the Belgae. They were conquered by Julius Caesar's armies in 51 B.C. The Roman province of Belgica was much larger than present-day Belgium.

Following the Roman Empire's collapse, Belgica was colonized by tribes from Germany in the third century A.D. It was later incorporated into the Holy Roman Empire until the ninth century A.D. Subse-

quently, Belgium became part of the kingdom of Lorraine.

Following the breakup of Lorraine in the eleventh century, several small provinces grew up around cities in what was to be Belgium. In 1384, the entire region came under the control of the Duke of Burgundy.

In 1477, through intermarriage, the Belgian provinces passed to the control of Emperor Charles V of the Austriam Habsburg family. When he abdicated the throne in 1555 they went to his son, King Philip II of Spain.

The rapidly growing Protestant population turned against the Catholic Spaniards in 1568. For the next eighty years the area was locked in a war with Spain. The death toll was horrendous and the fighting drained the region's resources. The Netherlands broke from Spain, but the Belgian area remained under its authority.

The Spanish Habsburg line of monarchs ended in the late 1600s. A war for Spain's throne followed. The region once again passed to Austrian Habsburg control in 1713. France occupied the region during the revolutionary wars. The Treaty of Formio confirmed France's possession in 1797.

Belgium

Britain defeated Napoleon's French armies at the Battle of Waterloo in 1815. Belgium was subsequently placed under Dutch control. This led to a rebellion in 1830 and the declaration of Belgium as an independent country. The Dutch King William I ordered his forces to retake the territory. They were forced to withdraw when France and Britain sided with Belgium.

Belgian independence was confirmed at the London Conference of 1830–31. When the new country decided it was to be a monarchy, Prince Leopold of Saxe-Coburg-Gotha was chosen as king. With the 1839 Treaty of London, the major European powers guaranteed Belgium's neutrality.

Its security confirmed, Belgium embarked on a program of major industrial development. It led much of Europe in the creation of new industries. Railway construction, heavy engineering works and coal mining featured prominently.

Under the rule of King Leopold II, from 1865 to 1909, Belgium became a colonial power. It formally annexed a large region of Africa known as the Congo. The Belgian Congo was the possession of the king, to use as he wished. The colony was ruthlessly exploited. Land was taken from the indigenous people who were also recruited as forced laborers. Protests in Belgium as well as in other countries forced the king to give control of the Congo to the parliament.

Germany invaded Belgium at the outset of World War I in 1914. It provided the shortest route to attack France. This clear violation of the 1839 Treaty of London brought Britain to Belgium's defense. By October 10, 1914, most of the country was occupied by Germany. The only exception was the battlefield of Ypres in West Flanders. It remained the front line, the scene of millions of casualties, until 1918. German atrocities in Belgium strongly affected the decision of the United States to enter the war in 1917. The Treaty of Versailles officially ended the war. The treaty stated that Germany would surrender lands to Belgium as well as monetary payments to aid in rebuilding the country.

The Second World War saw Germany again invade Belgium, in 1939. This time it was far more successful. The whole of Belgium, and subsequently France, fell to the German onslaught. On May 28, 1940, Belgium formally surrendered. King Leopold III was taken prisoner.

Most of the country was liberated by United States and British forces in September of 1944. On Belgian soil, German forces staged a counter-attack

An example of the devastation suffered by southern Belgium during World War I, 1914–18.

ELECTRA COLLECTION

FLAT EARTH PICTURE GALLERY

Street cafés in Antwerp, Belgium's famous diamond center.

known as the Battle of the Bulge. It lasted from December of 1944 to January of 1945, adding considerably to the damage already done to the country.

After the war, Belgium's industries were restored much faster than in the rest of Europe. Recovery was greatly assisted by millions of dollars worth of aid under the United States' Marshall Plan.

Further economic stability came from the formation of the Benelux Economic Union in 1948. Comprising Belgium, Netherlands and Luxembourg, Benelux provided a template for the later creation of the European Union. The capital city, Brussels, was chosen in 1949 as headquarters for the North Atlantic Treaty Organization (NATO).

The role of King Leopold during the war caused great debate. His decision to order the army to surrender was widely criticized. Officially

barred from returning to Belgium, in 1951 he abdicated in favor of his son Baudouin.

The Belgian Congo saw bloody pro-independence riots during 1959. Alarmed by this, Belgium abruptly granted independence the following year. They had done little to prepare the Congo for the change. A bloody civil war erupted as various groups jockeyed for control. In Belgium there was economic turmoil and bitter political recriminations.

Throughout the 1960s tensions grew between the Dutch- and French-speaking sections of the population. In an attempt to placate both sides, three semi-autonomous regions were created in the 1970s. They were Dutch-speaking Flanders, French-speaking Wallonia and a separate territory for Brussels, the capital city. This was further refined into a federal structure in 1993. That same year King Baudouin died and was succeeded by his brother Albert.

The cultural divisions within Belgium make cooperation difficult. At the beginning of the 2000s, the economy of Flanders was strong. However, the people of Wallonia suffered hardship from high unemployment. Leaders are hoping that a stronger central government will help all areas to benefit from a great capacity to work together in the future.

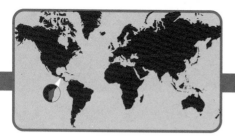

Belize

Belize is located in Central America, on the Caribbean Sea between Mexico and Guatemala. Its landscape varies from swampy coastal plains to the Maya Mountains in the south. Much of its very flat land is made up of forest areas. Off the coast of Belize, in the Caribbean Sea, is the world's second-largest coral reef. The climate is tropical with the temperature ranging only slightly throughout the year.

Close to half of the population is mestizo, those with mixed Spanish and indigenous backgrounds. The other dominant group is of African-European descent. Mayans, who make up about ten percent of the population, live in the interior. Belize is largely Christian. English is the official language, but about a third of the people speak Spanish.

Archeologists have uncovered evidence of agricultural activity between 2500 and 1100 B.C. The first known inhabitants, dating from 1800 B.C., were the Mayan and the Carib. It is believed that Spanish conquistadors of the 1500s claimed the land, making it a part of Guatamela. However, they built no settlements. In the early 1600s, British sailors began the first settlement.

When Jamaica-based companies began exploiting Belize's fine timbers, Britain assumed control. Spain disputed this claim in a number of clashes during the 1700s. The region became the crown colony of British Honduras, under the control of Jamaica, in 1862. It was made an independent colony in 1884.

A general election in 1954 brought limited self-government. Independence was slow in coming because Guatemala tried to enforce its early claim to the area. Britain granted full self-government in 1964.

British Honduras became Belize in 1973. Its new capital city was Belmopan. Independence was proclaimed on September 21, 1981. A parliamentary democracy, Belize retains the British monarch as head of state.

Guatemala refused to recognize the new country's indepence. About 1,500 British troops occupied the island to protect the new government from the threat of Guatemalan interference. Guatemala officially recognized the independence of Belize in 1991.

At this time, the economy of Belize is not strong. It exports fruit, sugar, fish, as well as woods such as mahogany and cedar. It is still a developing nation reliant upon financial aid from other countries. Belize is striving to strengthen its tourist industry, while curbing local involvement in illegal drug shipments from Colombia to the United States.

GOVERNMENT
Website www.belize.gov.bz
Capital Belmopan
Type of government
Parliamentary democracy
Independence from Britain
September 21, 1981
Voting Universal adult suffrage
Head of state
British Crown,
represented by Governor-General
Head of government
Prime Minister
Constitution 1981
Legislature
Bicameral parliament
House of Representatives (lower
house), Senate (upper house)
Judiciary Supreme Court
Member of Caricom, CN, IMF,
OAS, UN, UNESCO, WHO, WTO

LAND AND PEOPLE
Land area 8,867 sq mi
(22,965 sq km)
Highest point Victoria Peak
3530 ft (1160 m)
Coastline 240 mi (386 km)
Population 262,999
Major cities and populations
Belize City 53,000
Orange Walk 15,500
Belmopan 8,500
Ethnic groups
Mestizo 45%, African-European
30%, Mayan 10%
Religion Christianity
Languages English (official)

ECONOMIC
Currency Belizean dollar
Industry
clothing, food processing, tourism
Agriculture
bananas, coca, citrus,
sugar cane, timber
Natural resources
timber, seafood

Benin

REPUBIC OF BENIN

GOVERNMENT
Capital Porto-Novo
Seat of government Cotonou
Type of government Republic
Independence from France
August 1, 1960
Voting Universal adult suffrage
Head of state President
Head of government President
Constitution 1990
Legislature
Unicameral National Assembly
Judiciary Constitutional Court
Member of IMF, OAU, UN,
UNESCO, WHO, WTO

LAND AND PEOPLE
Land area 44.300 sq mi
(114,760 sq km)
Highest point
Mont Sokbaro 213 m (658 m)
Coastline 75 mi (121 km)
Population 6,787,625
Major cities and populations
Cotonou 550,000
Porto-Novo 180,000
Djougou 140,000
Ethnic groups
Fon 40%, others 60%
Religions
Indigenous faiths 60%,
Christianity 15%, Islam 15%,
Languages
French (official),
numerous indigenous languages

ECONOMIC
Currency CFA franc
Industry
textiles, food processing, chemicals,
construction materials
Agriculture
cotton, corn, tapioca, yams, beans,
palm oil, peanuts, livestock
Natural resources
limestone, marble, timber

Extending north from the Gulf of Guinea, Benin is a narrow country in western Africa. Most of the narrow coastal plain is cultivated as farm land This area gives way to a rocky central plateau. The Niger River forms part of the boundary with the Republic of Niger. Benin's climate is tropical with distinct wet and dry seasons.

Benin has more than fifty different ethnic groups. The largest is the Fon, who along with the Adja, whose culture is very similar, make up about half of the country' residents. . Other dominant groups are the Bariba and the Yoruba.

A majority of the people practic traditional animist religions. Animism is based on the idea that all elements in nature have spirits. Voodoo, one type of animism is most prevalent. Christians and Muslims make up about thirty percent of the people. French is the official language, but ethnic languages are most commonly used.

The kingdom of Great Ardra was founded in present-day Benin in the twelfth century A.D. In 1625, a dispute split the kingdom into many smaller realms. Abomey was one of more prosperous new kingdoms. Its king captured other coastal kingdoms during the 1700s.

France wanted to annex much of the region in the late 1800s. The Dahomey Empire resisted but France was victorious. It was named a part of French West Africa in 1904.

Independence came to Dahomey on August 1, 1960. Instability and unrest led to many abrupt changes in the government. In October, 1972, Major Mathieu Kérékou, a follower of Marxist philosophy, seized control. He renamed Dahomey the People's Republic of Benin in 1975.

Industries were nationalized, all other political parties were banned, and aid was sought from communist countries. However, continued unrest and an attemped military coup led Kérékou to renounce Marxism in 1989. He vowed to participate in formal a more liberal government. In 2001, Kérékou was once again reelected.

Unrest in neighboring countries led more than 150,000 refugees to arrive in Benin in 1993. Severe hardship caused about two-thirds of them to leave within two years.

Benin remains a very poor country. About two-thirds of its people work as farmers, growing only enough food to live. The country's health and educational systems are weak. One in ten children dies at birth, while many others don't live to adolescence. Fewer than thirty percent of the people can read and write.

Bhutan

KINGDOM OF BHUTAN

Mountainous Bhutan is located between China and India. The Greater Himalaya range reaches a height of 24,471 feet (7553 m) in the northern part of the country. The south is dominated by fertile valleys and semi-tropical forests, drained by major rivers. Much of the northern mountain area is permanently snow-bound. Temperatures in lower-lying areas range from 40°F (4°C) in January to 80°F (27°C) mid-year.

Only five percent of the people live in urban areas. Sixty-five percent of the people are of Kuamas Bhutia or Bhote descent. Most of these people live in the north. The south is inhabited by Gurung, Nepalese, Bhutia Monpa and Sherdukpen peoples. About seventy percent of the people follow Lamaistic Buddhism, the state religion. Most of the remainder are Hindus. More than half of the adult population is illiterate.

Farming and the wood products industries employ most working adults. The national focus on ecology strictly protects the natural beauty. Tourism is limited to a very large extent out of concern for the environment.

The original people came from Tibet in the ninth century A.D. These were the forebears of today's dominant group, the Bhotia (a name derived from Bod, the ancient name for Tibet). Civil and religious leaders had formed a shared monarchy by the sixteenth century. Following a dispute between Bhutan and Bengal in 1772, the British East India Company sent troops to control the situation. Britain annexed the region in 1865. It served as a sort of buffer state for British India.

A monarchy was established in 1907. Britain granted it internal autonomy. The provincial governor, Ugyen Wangchuk, was the first king. Britain supported Bhutan financially and controlled its foreign relations. Newly-independent India took over this role in 1949.

King Jigme Dorji Wangchuk came to power in 1953. He reformed land ownership, abolished slavery and the caste system, and emancipated women. King Jigme Singye Wangchuk, crowned in 1974, handed over government to a cabinet and partly-elected legislature, the Tshogdu. The legislature confirm its confidence in the king by a poll taken every three years.

Progressive groups have campaigned to see the government made more liberal. Many people fled to other countries during the 1990s, charging the government with human rights abuses. Most recently, tension developed with Nepal and India when Bhutan expelled thousands of Nepalese as illegal immigrants.

GOVERNMENT
Capital Thimphu
Type of government
Absolute monarchy
Independence from British influence
August 8, 1949
Voting
One vote per family for village level elections only
Head of state Monarch
Head of government
Chairman of the Council of Ministers
Constitution 1981
Legislature
Unicameral National Assembly (Tshogdu), partially elected
Judiciary High Court
Member of
IMF, UN, UNESCO, WHO

LAND AND PEOPLE
Land area 18,150 sq mi (47,000 sq km)
Highest point Kula Kangri 24,471 ft (7553 m)
Population 2,094 176
Major cities and populations
Thimphu 34,000
Phuntsholing 27,000
Ethnic groups Kuamas Bhutia 65%, Gurung 15%, others 20%
Religions
Buddhism 70%, Hinduism 25%, Islam 5%
Languages
Dzongkha (official), Lhotsan, English

ECONOMIC
Currency Ngultrum
Industry
cement, wood products, fruits, beverages, calcium carbide
Agriculture
rice, corn, root crops, citrus fruits, dairy
Natural resources
timber, gypsum, calcium carbide

Bolivia

REPUBLIC OF BOLIVIA

GOVERNMENT
Website www.ine.gov.bo
Capital La Paz
Type of government Republic
Independence from Spain
August 6, 1825
Voting
Universal adult suffrage, compulsory
Head of state President
Head of government President
Constitution 1967, revised 1994
Legislature
Bicameral National Congress
Chamber of Deputies (lower house)
Chamber of Senators (upper house)
Judiciary Supreme Court
Member of
IMF, OAS, UN, UNESCO, WHO, WTO

LAND AND PEOPLE
Land area 424,164 sq mi
(1,098,581 sq km)
Highest point
Nevada Illampu 21,196 ft (6,542 m)
Population 8,445,134
Major cities and populations
La Paz 1,100,000
Santa Cruz de la Sierra 1,100,000
Cochabamba 600,000
Oruru 230,000
Ethnic groups
Mestizo 30%, Quechua 25%,
European 15%, other indigenous 30%
Religion
Christianity 95%,
Languages
Spanish, Aymara, Quechua
(all official)

ECONOMIC
Currency Boliviano
Industry
mining, smelting, petroleum,
food, beverages, clothing
Agriculture
soybeans, coffee, coca, cotton, corn,
sugar cane, rice, potatoes, timber
Natural resources
tin, natural gas, petroleum, zinc,
tungsten, antimony, silver, iron,
lead, gold, timber

Landlocked Bolivia lies in west central South America. Its geography is truly varied, with tall, rugged mountains in the west, semi-arid plains in the south and lush rain forests in the east. More than half the country is heavily forested. The vast Andes Range reaches its greatest width in Bolivia. There are two cordilleras, or mountain ranges, one on the Chilean border, the other in the center of the country. Both run north-south, enclosing the Altiplano, plateau 11,000 feet (3500 m) above sea level. The impressive Lake Titicaca lies in the north, on the border with Peru.

Bolivia's climate varies greatly, according to altitude. The northeastern rainforests are warm and damp. In contrast, drought conditions regularly prevail in the south during summer. Temperatures in the valleys are pleasantly warm in summer. Above 16,000 feet (500 m) conditions become close to arctic. The capital, La Paz, experiences maximum summer temperatures of around 54° F (12°C).

The majority of Bolivians live in urban areas on the Altiplano, although it is bleak and harsh. In terms of race, thirty percent of the population is mestizo, people of mixed Spanish and indigenous descent. Twenty-five percent are indigenous Quechua peoples. Fifteen percent are European, principally Spaniards. There are many other indigenous groups. Some live in isolated regions relatively uninfluenced by European culture.

There are three official languages. Spanish is the language of the mestizos, Aymara and Quechua, are spoken by indigenous groups. There are also dialects which combine all three languages. Christianity, particularly Catholicism, is the official religion. Indigenous peoples in the Altiplano retain their traditional belief systems. There are small groups of Protestants, mainly Methodists and Baptists, and a tiny Jewish minority.

Bolivia is one of the poorest

LONELY PLANET IMAGES – ERIC WHEATER

Bolivia

nations of South America. Much of its economy is based on subsistence farming. Coca, grown illegally for the manufacture of cocaine, is a popular crop because of the money it earns. Corn, soybeans, sugar cane, coffee, potatoes, wheat and rice are important legitimate crops. Timber harvesting is another key industry.

Bolivia's industry is limited, consisting mainly of smelting and oil refining. The country's abundant reserves of natural gas and oil have not been fully exploited. Extraction of antimony, bismuth, silver and lead forms a relatively small sector of the economy. The once-large tin mining industry has been affected by international competition.

Since independence in 1825, Bolivia has been blighted by almost 200 revolutions and *coups d'état*. The most recent

version of the constitution was adopted in 1967. It provides for a president elected directly by the people every four years. The legislature is bicameral, with a twenty-seven member Senate and a 130-member Chamber of Deputies.

It is generally believed that people lived in the Bolivian Andes 21,000 years ago. From the seventh to the thirteenth century A.D. the most developed culture was that of the Tiwanaku Indians in the north. Gradually, the Inca empire overcame them, ruling much of Bolivia for two hundred years.

Inca civilization was shattered in 1532 by the arrival of Spanish conquistadors led by Francisco Pizarro. By the 1540s the invaders had discovered the incredible wealth of Bolivia's silver mines. A large proportion of the indigenous population was brutally forced to work

there. Bolivia was administered by the Spanish viceroyalty of Peru from 1544 to 1824.

The plunder of Bolivia's riches and exploitation of its people continued unabated into the nineteenth century. Finally, in 1809, the people rose up against their oppressors at Chuquisaca. This independence movement was led by Simón Bolívar, from whose name Bolivia is taken. Final victory against the Spanish came in 1824 at the Battle of Ayacucho.

The Republic of Bolivia was proclaimed on August 6, 1825, with a constitution drawn up by Bolívar. Antonio José de Sucre, who led the forces against the Spanish, became the first president. After only three years he was forced to resign. His eccentric and ego-driven successors did little for Bolivia.

President Andrés Santa Cruz invaded Peru in 1836, intending to unite the two countries. Subsequent conflicts with other neighbors resulted in Bolivian territory being whittled away. Corruption was ever-present, especially in the management of the nation's mineral wealth.

In the twentieth century things grew worse. Military coups and brutal dictators led the country to bankruptcy.

LONELY PLANET IMAGES – ERIC WHEATER

Hillside housing in La Paz.

Desperate for economic help, Bolivia turned to international financiers. In the 1930s, a disastrous war with Paraguay over the Chaco region further weakened the economy.

Demand for Bolivian minerals during World War II helped stabilize its finances. At first the government sided with Germany. Following a revolution by miners, pro-German factions in the government were expelled. Bolivia joined the Allies. The revolutionary government ended in 1946 when its leader, Gualberto Villaroel, was hanged by a mob.

Conservative rule then lasted until 1951 when the National Revolutionary Movement (MNR) won the presidency. The military blocked it from taking power. Backed by the police and a militia comprised of miners and peasants, the MNR overthrew the military. It nationalized mining companies and improved social conditions. The MNR government lasted until 1964 when it was overthrown by a military *coup d'état*.

This pattern of elected governments interrupted by military coups continues to the present day. In the 1990s, under pressure from the United States, a campaign was launched to eradicate coca growing. This has led to civil unrest caused by great economic hardship in many regions.

LONELY PLANET IMAGES – DEANNA SWANEY

The tiny church at Quila Quila, high in the mountains.

Bosnia and Herzegovina

REPUBLIC OF BOSNIA and HERZEGOVINA

Bordered by Croatia and Yugoslavia, Bosnia and Herzegovina is an Eastern European nation. It is land-locked, except for a very narrow access corridor to the Adriatic Sea. Bosnia, in the northern region, is primarily mountains. Herzegovina, in the south, is mostly flat farmland interspersed with rocky hills. While Bosnia and Herzegovina has very cold, snowy winters, summers are temperate and pleasant.

Events of the 1990s affected Bosnia and Herzegovina's population dramatically. Until then, Bosnian Muslims represented a majority. However, as some fled while others were killed, Serbs and Croats became a dominant presence. Christianity, either Catholic or Serbian Orthodox, is the religion of nearly fifty percent of the people. Most of the remaining half are Muslims. The main language is Serbo-Croatian.

Agriculture was traditionally the mainstay of Bosnia and Herzegovina's economy. Since the civil war, production has fallen dramatically. Today, the country grows barely half its needs. Steel, textiles, timber products and machinery are the main manufactures.

The Roman Empire province of Illyricum included

Bosnia and Herzegovina. Slav tribes migrated to the region in the seventh century A.D. By the tenth century, Bosnia was semi-autonomous, with its own governor. During much of the next three hundred years, Hungary exercised control over either or both Bosnia and Herzegovina.

The Turkish Ottoman Empire conquered Bosnia in 1463 and Herzegovina in 1482. Many people subsequently converted to Islam. Jews expelled from Spain and Portugal flocked to Bosnia and Herzegovina.

Bosnia became a key Turkish outpost. Sarajevo was its

regional capital. Following the Russo-Turkish War of 1877–78, Austria occupied Bosnia-Herzegovina. It formally became part of the Austro-Hungarian Empire in 1908.

On June 28, 1914, a Bosnian Serb revolutionary assassinated Archduke Franz Ferdinand, of Austria-Hungary, in Sarajevo. This single act led to the terrible bloodshed of World War I. Austria-Hungary attacked Serbia. Germany and the Ottoman Empire joined Austria-Hungary against Serbia, Russia, France, and Britain.

The Austria-Hungarian Empire was defeated at the end of the war. Bosnia and

Returning refugees in temporary accommodation at Jelac.

Herzegovina were merged and became part of the Kingdom of Serbs, Croats, and Slovenes in 1918. The country was re-named the Kingdom of Yugoslavia in 1929. During World War II, it was made part of Croatia.

After the war, the former Croatian leader Josip Broz Tito established Yugoslavia as a communist federation. Bosnia and Herzegovina was included as a separate republic. Yugoslavia, largely independent of the Soviet Union, was a much more open society. Bosnia and Herzegovina became heavily industrialized. It was the center of Yugoslavia's arms industry. Throughout Yugoslavia, ethnic and religious tensions ran high among the different republics.

Yugoslavia began breaking up in the early 1990s. Initially, Bosnia and Herzegovina remained loyal. Threatened by a Serbian takeover in 1992, it opted for independence. Bosnia's Serb minority declared the Serbian Republic of Bosnia and Herzegovina in April, 1992.

Bosnian Serbs, led by Radovan Karadzic, captured |the weapons left behind by the Yugoslav army. Assisted by troops from Serbia, they isolated parts of Bosnia with majority Serb populations. The Muslim-held capital city of Sarajevo came under siege.

The European Union and the United Nations imposed trade sanctions on Serbia in May of 1992. The Serbs' ethnic cleansing policy led thousands of Muslims to massacre or placement in detention camps. Muslim-held cities were all but destroyed by Serbian shelling. The situation deteriorated in 1995. Incidents of rape and civilian killings were common-place. The worst occurred at Srebrenica.

Peace talks between Bosnian Muslims, Croats, and Serbians were held in Dayton, Ohio, in late 1995. The result was an agreement for a Bosnian repub-lic with two semi-autonomous regions. One was for Serbs, the other for Muslims and Croats. A NATO force of 60,000 troops would keep the peace until June 1998.

The situation has calmed significantly, but distrust and suspicion remains widespread. Peacekeepers remain, although the numbers are now less than 20,000. Parliamentary elections were held in November of 2000. A moderate coalition led by the multiethnic Alliance for Change took office three months later. In August, 2001, a United Nations tribunal found Serbian general Radislav Krstic guilty of genocide. He had com-manded the massacre of 7,000 people at Srebrenica.

GOVERNMENT
Website www.fbihvlada.gov.ba
Capital Sarajevo
Type of government Republic
Voting Universal adult suffrage
Head of state
Chairman of the Presidency
Head of government
Chairman of the Council
of Ministers
Constitution 1995
Legislature
Bicameral Parliamentary
Assembly (Skupstina)
National House of Representatives
(Predstavnicki Dom)
House of Peoples (Dom Naroda)
Judiciary Constitutional Court
Member of
IMF, UN, UNESCO, WHO

LAND AND PEOPLE
Land area 19,741 sq mi
(51,129 sq km)
Highest point Maglic
7,731 ft (2386 m)
Population 3,964,388
Major cities and populations
Sarajevo 550,000
Banja Luka 200,000
Zenica 160,000
Ethnic groups
Bosniak 44%, Serb 31%,
Croat 17%, Yugoslav 6%
Religions Christianity 50%,
Islam 40%
Languages Serbo-Croatian

ECONOMIC
Currency Marka
Industry
steel, mining,, textiles, wooden
furniture, aircraft assembly
appliances, oil refining
Agriculture
wheat, corn, fruits,
vegetables; livestock
Natural resources
coal, iron, bauxite, manganese,
timber, copper, chromium,
lead, zinc

Botswana

REPUBLIC OF BOTSWANA

Botswana is located in southern Africa. Most of it lies on the Southern African Plateau which runs north to south, averaging a height of 3,240 feet (1000 m) above sea level. In the south is the Kalahari Desert, while the Okavango River delta dominates the northwest. Rainfall is erratic, leading to regular droughts. Otherwise, the climate is subtropical.

The majority of the people are either Tswanas or Kalangas. Several differing Tswana peoples maintain a specific cultural identity. The San, who inhabit the Kalahari, are another significant minority. Seventy percent of the people follow traditional indigenous religions. The rest are mainly Protestant Christian. English is the official language, but most people speak Setswana the native language.

The region was originally settled by the San. In the seventeenth century they were gradually displaced by the Tswana. When the Zulu nation attempted to colonize the area in the 1820s, the Tswanas were successful at repelling them.

The first Europeans arrived in 1801, followed in 1813 by the London Missionary Society. The region became the center of attention in 1867 when gold was discovered near the Tati River.

The region, now called Bechuanaland became a British protectorate after the 1884-85 Conference of Berlin. The introduction of apartheid in 1948 ended any chance of Britain giving Bechuanaland to South Africa.

There was no strong movement toward freedom, but people who had served overseas during World War II came home with ideas for change. Independence was granted on September 30, 1966. Bechuanaland was renamed Botswana. The first president was Seretse Khama. The government, in the hands of Democratic Party since that time, remains stable.

Botswana was heavily dependent upon South Africa economic and technological aid in the years following its independence. It opposed the racial policies of South African governments prior to the 1990s, yet maintained close ties with the country out of necessity. Since the 1970s, it has been developing stronger farming, livestock processing, and mining industries. Its diamond reserves, among the largest in the world, hold great future economic promise.

Of particular concern at the present time is control of the virus which causes AIDS. More than thirty percent of its people are HIV-positive, giving Botswana the highest percentage of HIV-AIDS infection of any country in the world.

GOVERNMENT
Website www.gov.bw/home.html
Capital Gaborone
Type of government Republic
Independence from Britain
September 30, 1966
Voting Universal adult suffrage
Head of state President
Head of government President
Constitution 1966
Legislature
Bicameral Parliament
National Assembly (lower house)
House of Chiefs (upper house)
Judiciary High Court
Member of
CN, IMF, OAU, UN,
UNESCO, WHO, WTO

LAND AND PEOPLE
Land area 224,607 sq mi
(581,730 sq km)
Highest point Tsodilo Hills
4,824 ft (1489 m)
Population 1,591,232
Major cities and populations
Gaborone 192,000
Francistown 80,000
Serowe 62,000
Selebi-Phikwe 57,000
Ethnic groups
Tswana 75%, San 15%, others 10%
Religions
Traditional animist 70%,
Christian 28%
Languages
English, Sestswana (both official)

ECONOMIC
Currency Pula
Industry
mining, textiles
Agriculture
livestock, sorghum, maize, millet,
beans, sunflowers, groundnuts
Natural resources
diamonds, copper, nickel, salt, soda
ash, potash, coal, iron ore, silver